KT-440-714

EFFECTIVE SOLUTIONS FOR EVERYDAY CHALLENGES

101

TIPS FOR PARENTS
of Children with
AUTISM

Arnold Miller and Theresa C. Smith
Foreword by Dr. Paul J. Callahan
Afterword by Ethan B. Miller

Jessica Kingsley *Publishers*
London and Philadelphia

First published in 2014
by Jessica Kingsley Publishers
73 Collier Street
London N1 9BE, UK
and
400 Market Street, Suite 400
Philadelphia, PA 19106, USA

www.jkp.com

Library of Congress Cataloging in Publication Data
Miller, Arnold, 1927-
  101 tips for parents of children with autism : effective solutions for everyday challenges / Arnold Miller
and Theresa Smith ; foreword by Dr. Paul J. Callahan ; afterword by Ethan B. Miller.
    pages cm
  Includes bibliographical references and index.
  ISBN 978-1-84905-960-2 (alk. paper)
  1. Parents of autistic children. 2. Autistic children--Care. 3. Autistic children--Fam-
ily relationships. 4.
  Autism in children--Miscellanea. I. Smith, Theresa. II. Title.
  RJ506.A9M548 2014
  618.92'85882--dc23
                                    2013026745

British Library Cataloguing in Publication Data
A CIP catalogue record for this book is available from the British Library

ISBN 978 1 84905 960 2
eISBN 978 0 85700 818 3

Printed and bound in Great Britain

¡La lucha continua!

Parents, grandparents, caregivers, family and friends of children with autism everywhere: This book is for you.

CONTENTS

FOREWORD

I first met Arnold Miller on a hot day in June, 1991. Newly out of graduate school, I was hoping for a chance to do something important in my field. Little about the tired, red brick building housing the LCDC suggested it would provide such an opportunity, but Dr. Miller greeted me with energy and enthusiasm, appearing not to notice either the heat or the surroundings.

Of the impressions from that day, I recall most his ability to see in disordered children the as yet undiscovered foundations upon which so much could be built. He appeared to recognize what no one else could, and knew, with uncanny clarity, the right place to begin with them. In the many years we worked together, I witnessed countless examples of his vision, sometimes confounding or contradicting others', but nearly always containing a vital truth that became the bedrock of subsequent treatment.

He never saw cause for despair and was unfailing in his readiness to help another family find hope for meaningful progress in their child's development.

The inspiration to always look further and deeper into the language, behavior, and spirit of each client I see has remained with me and is a gift I will treasure always.

Graciously contributed by Dr. Paul J. Callahan, Psy.D., developmental therapist, for nearly two decades Deputy Director of the Language and Cognitive Development Center (LCDC), gifted therapist and advisor, and our friend for nearly as long.

PROLOGUE

It is a challenge and a privilege to work with the words of an eminent man who can no longer correct my mistakes.

The inspiration for this book is all Dr. Miller's. We had begun work on it during his final illness. To propagate his insights, I am taking the liberty of finishing this handbook.

Dr. Miller's perspective was that of a clinical professional, treating childhood autism through the instruments of skilled teachers, collaborators, speech therapists, and occupational therapists. He necessarily worked at one remove from the severely autistic young children to whom he devoted his professional life.

I do not.

We parents are down in the dirt, wrestling with what autism has done to our children. We call its name, we defy it, we grab it by the throat. This book reflects that removal of critical distance, and elimination of clinical nomenclature.

The basic materials are Dr. Miller's worksheets, collected writings, emails, personal correspondence, and video instructions when he worked as a developmental therapist for my son Benjamin. Many of the examples, and all the biographical intermezzi, arose in our lives with Ben.

In a far-too-generous offer of his time, Dr. Paul J. Callahan has reviewed this manuscript.

Any remaining errors are all mine.

Theresa Smith
dr.theresasmith@gmail.com

1

REACHING CHILDREN ON THE AUTISM SPECTRUM WITH THE MILLER METHOD®

Coping in an inconstant world[1]

Parents, caregivers of all stripes, friends, family, and loved ones, do you reach out every day to someone dear to you: a child with autism? This book is for you.

Profoundly disordered children on the autism spectrum are often intimidating to the parents who live with them and the professionals who try to help them. Faced with the range of unusual behavior the children display, parents often ask themselves, "Where do I start?" Complicating things further, your child is appealing, even beautiful, but may behave as if you do not exist. You yearn to elicit some kind of response—a fleeting glance, a smile—anything that communicates that you are more than wallpaper for that child. But your child may not permit this, or may not be able to reciprocate. As many parents put it, "You knock…but no one answers."

The common second reaction to these children is to rationalize the disorder. After all, it is painful to confront abnormality in a beloved child—you naturally want to make it go away. As a result, at first many parents and professionals

---

1 This discussion in a different form appears in Dr. Miller's book *The Miller Method®: Developing the Capacities of Children on the Autism Spectrum* (2007), and is printed here with the generous permission of the publisher, Jessica Kingsley.

may explain away the child's difficulty with change or with following directions, as simply "being stubborn," and may describe resistance to including others in their play as being due to the child's independent nature. Sometimes, even now, pediatricians—asked by anxious parents about their child's failure to communicate—may advise families not to worry, since, "After all, Einstein didn't speak until he was four."

Of course, a child may begin talking late for good reasons which are natural and do not warrant concern. If the parents speak more than one language at home, for example, their child will often begin to speak later than usual. But if your child *loses* speech, or any other ability, you want him evaluated immediately.

At the more severe end of the autism continuum, children may flap their arms and twiddle fingers in front of their faces, run in circles or from wall to wall in a room, flick lights on and off, flush toilets persistently, line things up, climb on furniture, and get lost inside the house or a short distance away. Verbal children may echo commercials from radio and television, or repeat what is said to them. Often, too, they demonstrate clumsiness, little reactivity to pain, or an uncertain sense of their own bodies. At the LCDC, in schools and homes, and in their private practices, Dr. Arnold Miller, Eileen Eller-Miller, Dr. Paul Callahan, Kristine Chrétien, and their capable teachers and therapists dealt with these challenges for decades. Over these years, Dr. Miller came to believe that to be effective it is essential to see our children as they are—not as we would like them to be.

Our observations can tell us much about the children's developmental obstacles, and about conditions which can be improved with teaching, therapy, and medical treatment. But Dr. Miller was a skeptical observer. Crediting the children with more capacity than they have is a serious error, Dr. Miller held, because it may result in beginning a treatment program that is beyond their reach, wasting precious time. Or it may cause a promising medical treatment to be overlooked. Remember that many therapies may be open to you.

Professionals sometimes say, as they observe the performance of a child with an autism spectrum disorder (ASD), "If it walks like a duck, and quacks like a duck, it *is* a duck." In other words, many practitioners believe that if the child provides the outer forms of typical functioning in her conduct, her speech, or her reading, then that child fully understands what she is doing, saying, or reading. Unfortunately, Dr. Miller witnessed far too many special children who *seemed* to be acting appropriately, using perfectly articulated speech or apparently reading, without having a clue about the meaning of what they were doing, saying, or reading. Wanting to create real competence, communication and comprehension, instead of their hollow shells, Dr. Miller rejected the duck analogy vigorously.

Consequently, we see in Miller Method® programs, Dr. Miller's insistence that children unambiguously demonstrate their full understanding in different contexts before moving on to a new task. Exceptions emerge in developing latent signs and other forms of early communication, which we encourage you to capture and accept as real and meaningful even as your child is becoming aware of them.

On the other hand, many parents' experience is more complex. They think their children with autism juggle their abilities, thoughts, and skills, and may sometimes drop the ball, not because the children are not proficient jugglers, but because a sensory distortion intervenes, or a neural connection is temporarily unavailable. These conditions shift, fog-like, and inhibit a sound evaluation of the child. Parents have concluded from their own observations that children with autism may know far more than they are able to reveal, especially within strict time limits. With patience and the right pacing, they will be able to show you. This means that it may be difficult or even impossible for the most severely affected children to demonstrate 100 percent mastery of any tasks, including those the child knows completely, just as fluent native speakers still occasionally make mistakes while speaking their mother tongue. Working and living with our autistic children, we always presume more competence, more capacity, more comprehension, and more intentionality that we can see. And that presumption can give rise to more competence.

What is autism and how has it been treated?

Autism is a neurological disorder of complex origin which affects a child's ability to process information from his own body or from surroundings.[2] It also interferes with a child's ability to play and to communicate. Your autistic child may have any one of a complex array of sensory and body movement planning neurological obstacles to surmount, including loss of speech or other abilities, reduced body awareness, and reduced pain sensitivity.

Because children with autism exhibit this array of sensory and motor-planning issues (Bogdashina 2004), they may find it difficult to gain full control over their bodies, and they may be hyper- or hypo-sensitive. Some children who are hypersensitive to sound find being in a noisy classroom or gym so painful that they need to cover their ears, run away, create a distraction, or even injure themselves in desperation. Other hypersensitive children may find it distressing to be

---

2   Among risk factors supported by research are heredity, environmental contamination, diet, and exposure to viruses. Heredity appears not to be decisive since cases of identical twins can be found in which only one has acquired autism, for example the Hallmayer *et al.* 2011 Stanford study.

touched. Many children on the spectrum have sensitivities to clothing, the flavors or texture of food, or strong smells. Hair brushing, haircuts, nail trimming, and tooth brushing may be excruciating experiences for them.

In contrast, some hyposensitive children—although having perfectly normal hearing—seem oblivious to spoken words or even loud noises. Many such children may fall and skin their knees or bump their heads and yet fail to cry or locate the source of the injury, due to irregularities in perception of pain and in body awareness.[3]

Unusual sensitivities, as well as extreme lack of sensitivity, may mean that our children suffer from impaired transmission of sensation from various parts of the body to the brain. Sensory irregularities also may mean that the normal two-way communication of muscles to brain and brain back to muscles, which maintains muscle tone, has been disrupted. These same transmission problems can pose problems for speaking, and appear to limit the children's ability to use their bodies adaptively in general. For example, the children may not have a clear sense of how one side of the body differs from the other, and as a result may be unable to climb over a fence. Or they have difficulty integrating the upper with the lower part of their bodies, and therefore cannot easily learn how to maneuver a tricycle around obstacles, or may have difficulty learning to crawl or swim. These difficulties reflect a striking lack of integrated body awareness which the children might try to compensate for by self-stimulatory body activity such as spinning and flapping hands, and by seeking "edge experiences" to help define and locate the body, allow fuller experience of body sensations, and offer reassurance. Verbal autistic young people report that climbing, standing

---

3   Some hyposensitivities may be caused by reactions to foods which create opiates; a special diet may help them.

in the shower, or lying in flowing water renews the sense of body awareness. Requiring such hyposensitive children to remain seated for extended periods of time may deaden them by depriving them of needed sensory input. Lack of sensory input may also provoke increased self-stimulation, self-injury, or even the very explosive behavior you seek to avoid. Such children benefit from outdoor activity, body contact sports, robust expression of affection within the family, intensive occupational therapy, and deep joint pressure. (Consult an occupational therapist with a specialization in autism for personalized help with your child's sensory irregularities.)

First described by Leo Kanner (1943, 1971) in its "pure" form—emphasizing impairment of the ability to make human contact—the syndrome is now understood as a continuum, Autism Spectrum Disorder (ASD), which ranges from the most withdrawn children to those who show some but not all the features Kanner initially described, perhaps in a mild form. *This book, like Dr. Miller's life work, is especially designed for those caring for young, pre-adolescent, more severely affected ASD children.*

The first approach in the 1950s to understanding the origins of autism was to presume autism was a psychiatric illness. Probably because the manifestations of autism superficially mirrored the state of known emotionally deprived and withdrawn infants, Bruno Bettelheim (1950) and other psychologists blamed distant "refrigerator" mothers for causing autism, by withholding nurturing from their children. These neglected children rapidly improved with regular nurturing. Seeing some of the same kinds of behavior among autistic children, including massive orality, psychoanalytic therapists sought to treat the disorder by addressing the assumed deprivation. Dr. Miller remembered Dr. Joseph Weinreb, a prominent psychoanalyst who directed the Worcester Youth Guidance Center for over a decade, feeding candy to children with autism from his "breast" pockets to treat the assumed oral deprivation of the children.

In the early 1960s the emotional deprivation view was replaced by a behavioral understanding derived from learning theory and based on B.F. Skinner's (1951) findings in animal experiments. Ivar Lovaas (1987) was one of the foremost proponents of the behaviorally derived Applied Behavior Analysis (ABA) approach. At about the same time, Dr. and Mrs. Miller introduced their cognitive-developmental systems method with its roots in Heinz Werner's developmental theory (Miller and Eller-Miller 1989, 2000; Miller 1991). The Miller approach, described by the late lamented Dr. Stanley Greenspan, during a clinical consultation in Bethesda, MD, on 8 August 2000, as much more natural than ABA, is now most often referred to as the Miller Method®.

The ABA approach makes no assumptions about the sources of autism or the inner emotional life of the child. Workers simply address the children's undesired behavior with the tools of learning theory—"reinforcing" with rewards of candy, food, tokens, or praise desired behaviors and attempting to "extinguish" with turning away, "time out," or aversive procedures those behaviors viewed as unacceptable. The behaviorists assume that if they can get a disordered child to *behave* like typical children, then, indeed, that child would for all practical purposes *be* typical, and respond as typical children do. Since typical children learn from a teacher while seated at a table or a desk, behaviorists assume that children with autism also need to sit at a table or at desks and look at the therapist or teacher before they can be taught.

This is one of many presumptions we think simply do not work.

We now know that both Weinreb and typical ABA programing's well-intentioned efforts do not address the underlying physical problem. In recent years, studies of the brains of autistic people have shown discernible neuroanatomical anomalies that probably account for much of the atypical sensory processing and unusual behavior in autism.

So the question of what works, especially for early intervention, has assumed new urgency, as the incidence of autism around the world has grown rapidly in recent years. More than 40 years ago, the rate was believed to be about 4 in 10,000. Some estimates were as low as 1 in 40,000.

In 2012, the US Centers for Disease Control and Prevention (CDC) released estimates from 2008 data that among USA eight-year-olds, 1 in 88 children suffers from some form of autism. This reflects a 75 percent increase from 2002 and a 23 percent increase since 2006, according to the CDC. Boys are at much greater risk than girls; 1 in 54 boys but only ("only!") 1 in 252 girls was afflicted with an ASD in the 2008 CDC data. So, in the USA, boys are more than four and a half times more likely to suffer from autism than girls are.[4] Many risks and causative factors may be at work, perhaps in several sequences, accounting for varying types and severities of autism.

On March 20, 2013, the CDC released results of a new survey showing 1 child in 50 is on the autism spectrum in the USA. The UN reports that the incidence of autism in all regions of the world is high.[5]

---

4   Many factors may be involved, but one reason for the greater risk to boys may be the tendency of testosterone to bind with mercury, a central nervous system antagonist.

5   UNSG Ban Ki-moon, announcing the April 2, 2013 observance of World Autism Awareness Day, remarked, "This international attention is essential to address stigma, lack of awareness and inadequate support structures. Now is the time to work for a more inclusive society, highlight the talents of affected people and ensure opportunities for them to realize their potential." Secretary-General Ban Ki-moon Message for the World Autism Awareness Day 2013. Available at www.un.org/en/events/autismday/2013/sgmessage.

How does the Miller Method® compare with Applied Behavior Analysis?

The Miller Method® of cognitive development contrasts sharply with ABA:

1. Where ABA tries to divert or "extinguish" undesired behavior, the Miller Method® attempts to harness the power of autistic children's drives, compulsions, and obsessions, and transform them into useful, interactive exchanges which build resilience and communication. The Miller Method® treats our autistic children's need for completion as an asset, whose energy can be channeled to teach them.

2. Where ABA emphasizes ignoring or turning away from the child who is misbehaving or having a tantrum, or isolating her from other children, the Miller Method® emphasizes turning toward and re-engaging the child. Reach your child by increasing your interactions with her.

3. Where ABA requires the child to remain seated to learn, the Miller Method® assumes that children with autism learn best through action, movement, and concrete illustrations, because of the nature of their nervous systems. Your child's sensory needs may mean that he needs to move to learn, rather than being required to remain seated and still.

4. Where ABA tries to establish compliance with the help of food and praise rewards, the Miller Method® establishes repetitive routines (systems) which are persistently expanded, complicated, and disrupted to elicit spontaneous initiatives and to induce communication from the children. In this way the

routines of our autistic children begin to approximate the routines of normal life.

5. Finally, unlike ABA, the Miller Method® teaches our children to generalize their functioning appropriately, to shift comfortably from one location to another, and to use transitions to acquire symbolic capacity.

Compliance, coping, and capability

Some children with autism are compliant as long as the requests made of them follow a familiar, predictable course. However, an unexpected change, no matter how minor, in the familiar routine or environment can trigger a catastrophic loss of control. Your child may lose composure when a light bulb burns out, his mother changes clothes or takes a slightly different route to the store, or even when a new child comes into the classroom. Other ASD children can comply with requests and cope with change as long as all rules and expectations in one context change completely, at the same time, to a new and well-understood set ("the rules at Grandmother's house," "the rules at school"), so that no ambiguity occurs.

But we want to go far beyond compliance. While the ABA approach may sometimes achieve compliance, this emphasis on compliance is at odds with our children's need to cope in an unpredictable world and—equally importantly— with the kinds of biological, biochemical and neurological challenges these children experience. ABA does not provide a working repertoire for life, whereas Miller Method® approaches allow the child to build sets of routines which can become a repertoire of coping and communication skills throughout life.

Coping in everyday life as a child, and later, as an adult, requires flexibility and discernment, not merely obedience.

If a stranger offers a hand to our child, we do not want the child to compliantly take that hand. We want our children to discriminate between hands offered by special carers and those offered by strangers. Beyond this, we want our children to be able to cope with everyday changes without distress. Excessive emphasis on compliance may work *against* our children's ability to cope with change. But even more importantly, requiring some children with autism to behave and respond *as if they were typical children* may simply be impossible, since this demand ignores the significant neurological differences these children live with.

Dr. Miller's core view about treating and educating children with ASD remained consistent across his entire career, as described in the first book *From Ritual to Repertoire* (Miller and Eller-Miller 1989), and even more directly in *The Miller Method* (Miller with Chrétien 2007). He maintained that all children on the autism spectrum—no matter how withdrawn or disorganized—show a strong drive to find a way to cope with a confusing world in flux. Children with autism express this coping drive in spite of major challenges in experiencing their bodies, while tolerating intense sensory experiences that they have scant ability to screen out. Our task is to help our beloved children unlock all their capacities to live full, meaningful lives.

Tip # 1: Do not settle for the mere appearance of meaningful functioning.

In a classroom, we once saw a youngster with ASD correctly sort and identify by name eight colors. When taken outside and asked what color the sky was, he was clueless.

Tip # 2: Always presume capability. Always!

Intermezzo

Dilemma: OK, now, those first two tips look contradictory. How do we know which one to use when?

As human beings, we try to define our place in the vast, mysterious universe in which we live. We want to understand our nature and how we relate to other living things. We think about what came before us and what will come after…

…for all our limitations, we are nonetheless creatures of worth.

On this matter, the sages gave us excellent advice. They said that each person should carry two notes in his or her pockets. On one would be the words, "For my sake the world was created." On the other, "I am but dust and ashes." When we despair of our value, we look at the first. When we are too haughty, we look at the second.[6]

---

6   Rabbi Dr. Reuven Hammer (2005), from *Entering the High Holy Days*. Published by the Jewish Publication Society and reprinted in "From Rosh Hashanah to Yom Kippur" at www.myjewishlearning.com/holidays/Jewish_Holidays/ Rosh_Hashanah/High_Holidays/Ten_Days/Rosh_Hashanah_to_Yom_ Kippur.shtml.

2

HOW TO CAPTURE YOUR CHILD'S ATTENTION, INCREASE FOCUS, AND DEVELOP COPING SKILLS

Capturing attention

Your severely autistic child may need all possible clues to be able to orient to you, especially soon after the onset of autism. And he may enjoy intense stimulation, or require only delicate approaches.

If he enjoys heavy physical contact, give it to him!

Tip # 3a: Start with rough and tumble play, physically engaging your child.

You want to work your child up to an alert, aroused state to interact with you. Depending on your own child's needs and sensitivities, start with some whole body work that will amuse him and help him pay attention.

Rough and tumble play is the single most important, and probably most under-rated, method of waking up your child's intellect and helping his emotional ties to his family and friends develop and blossom. While you are playing, you offer direct vigorous and repetitive physical contact between parent and child, which creates repeated opportunities for your child to experience you and your affection. Keep up a happy, playful mood while you are engaging your child.

If you do not remember rough and tumble from your own childhood, try rolling your child playfully from side to side, commenting and narrating, "Daddy is rolling Evan! Ha ha!" Try bringing his knees up so he can push you away and experience that large muscle strength. If your child is small enough, try playing "airplane," by lying on your back on the floor, balancing your child on your feet, and holding his hands. You can make airplane noises as you take off and land.

Also, try tossing a smaller child into the air and catching him, or tossing a larger child over a soft landing spot like a sofa and letting her drop. You can also swing your child, and bounce her up and down on a trampoline or a large ball while holding her hands. Accompany the bouncing with rhythmic narration: "Up, up, Natalie goes! And where she stops, Natalie knows!"

Pillow fights can be fun; also try wrestling. Try a horse ride in which you are the horse. Try bouncing your small child on your knee, while pretending she is riding a pony. If you are outside and you are strong enough, sling your child up on your shoulders and trot around, always holding her hands so that she doesn't slip. Or carry her in a baby backpack, securely strapped in.

If your child is not overly sensitive to sound, use rewarding exclamations like "Hurrah! Yay!" often as you are rough-housing.

Play "Ben Ball" with your Ben: while you are all standing, push him toward his mother, who exclaims, "Yes, I want him!" As he arrives at his mother's side, you demand him back. "No! I want him," at which point she pushes him in your direction.

Try deep pressure and massage; try setting your child in your lap and compressing her firmly in an affectionate embrace; try ticking, and anticipatory tickling, in which you announce "I am going to tickle your RIBS!" etc.

Although some experts think this is impossible, some children with autism can tickle their own ribs.

Include deep pressure for increasing focus and time on task during your rough-housing sessions. A severely autistic child may need intense deep pressure to be able to focus and communicate with you. A small child can give himself this pressure if you demonstrate how, or if you make some pressure-yielding activities look like fun. Make this sensory diet a regular part of your day, like eating. When you have carried out a pressure-producing routine, you are more likely to have an attentive child ready to relate to you. Parents report several tactics that have worked for them, including rhythmic actions that look like dance steps. For example:

Have your Nathan stamp his left foot, stamp his right foot, flex his legs, slap his left knee with his right hand, slap his right knee with his left hand, and clap his hands twice. Preferably do this hard enough to shake the floor. Narrate what you are doing, and do it WITH Nathan; sing, play music, to add sensation. Cheer at the end, if it doesn't disturb your Nathan.

This set of actions serves the additional incidental purpose of having Nathan cross the midline of his body, which is difficult for many ASD children but aids development because it increases communication between the hemispheres of the brain. Routines like this one also help satisfy sensory hunger by feeding in loud sounds and the floor vibrations created by stamping.

Tip # 3b: To increase focus, rough-house with your sensory craving child before a reading session or other play or work time at home, squeeze him between two gym mats ("Ben sandwich"), press him firmly and repeatedly into the doorframe with your shoulder while saying playfully "Excuse me, Ben!"[1]

Be mindful that you must choose your rough and tumble contact with your beloved Ben according to his sensory needs and tolerance. He may crave contact and jostling, a firm galloping bounce on your knee or hip, if he is small, yet only be able to tolerate small amounts at a time. If so, let him run away. He will be back.

Other children require gentle body work with powders, lotions, or large cosmetic brushes to wake up their skin.

You can increase focus and body awareness by pulling on your child's extremities, gently, and with narration and comment. Have her lie down with an adult at her head and feet, or on either side; adults narrate and can yell, "I want these hands!" "Oh, throw these dirty feet away!" as they are pulling on hands and feet. An occupational therapist may suggest you try to sustain the pulling for a few seconds.

Always keep looking for new ways to meet your child's need for deep pressure, since some methods may lose effectiveness over time or with frequent use.

Tip # 3c: You will increase your Ben's time on task if you can continue to satisfy his sensory hunger during the task.

If your Ben is very visual, continually surveys the places he is in, and responds happily to visual images, you may want to consider computer programs and applications which appeal

---

1   This example we owe to Christopher Idzerda.

to his interest in rapidly changing vivid images. One example is *Great Action Adventure*,[2] which can be set by parents and others to teach signing, reading, and receptive language (recognizing spoken words) using engaging sounds, short videos, and attractive photos. If Ben answers correctly by pointing with the computer mouse, he will see one of several dynamic images, a car racing loudly across the screen, three basketballs bounding toward him, a rocket launch, or a skier zipping down a slope.

If your Ben is very tactile, and needs to feel textures while he is working or looking at books, keep a large plastic jar about a third full of dry beans, lentils, corn, rice, marbles, strings of beads, or other small objects for him to feel. Encourage him to keep one hand in the jar, touching and holding the little objects, while he pays attention to other tasks. You can attach a fabric cuff to the edge of the jar to help keep the little items in the jar from bouncing out. (The cuff won't prevent throwing, but it will help minimize the amount that can be removed with a closed hand.)

If your son James needs a lot of tactile sensation but rice and beans options are not workable for him, you can try tidier choices such as heavily textured fabric, velvet, silk, sandpaper, horsehair, rubber bristles, and soft cosmetic brushes.

If your daughter Stephanie needs mild sensation, let her pat on some cornstarch, or play with some cornstarch

---

2   *Great Action Adventure* is one of the software options made by Silver Lining Multimedia, Inc., for visual learners. Their products are ideal for those with autism, brain injury, cerebral palsy (CP), Down Syndrome, developmental delays, aphasia, and other conditions requiring augmentative communication. Their photo software is also a great way to teach new words to English as a second language (ESL) and special education students. Many apps are offered for the iPad®, iPod®, and iPhone®, as well as computers. You can find them at www.silverliningmm.com.

Aunt Susan has combined with a little water, just so that the resulting putty flows, but will also break.

If music helps your Ken find continuity and stay on task, play something he likes in the background as he works, or let him control a radio, a CD player, an iPad®, or other device loaded with his favorite music. If your child craves music, let him listen to all music, not restricting him to only a few varieties thought to be age-appropriate. Perhaps your Ben loves Otis Redding best. Perhaps your Amy loves Heavy Metal. (OK, at their ages they will not follow the lyrics. But they may really need the complexities of sound, and may even crave symphonic music.)

As your child becomes more able to interact with you, he may still lose focus after only a short time. Surprises may help him focus on you, on the task at hand, on communication, and on re-establishing order.

Tip # 4a: Use the elements of drama and surprise.

Apply this idea inventively in many contexts.

Drama:

You can be a drama queen or king. Your child may respond well to exaggerated emotions, operatic gestures, strong facial expressions, expansive body movements, and a wide range of voice tones and volumes. Try them! As you vary your tone of voice, vary your vocabulary. Your child may at first find complex language perplexing; you may need to use minimal language for a while

You may find that your child attends to you better if you sing when you communicate with her, or if you whisper sometimes.

Also try surprises in the form of visual jokes. Parents note that appeals to humor often work to engage their child, increase their focus, and increase communication with us, as well as deepening our emotional ties. So, if your April is alert to what she sees, but is difficult to engage, reach her by creating a dramatic visual joke which needs to be straightened up.

If your young April likes to spend hours after school in the bathtub, you may alter the environment. One day, before she gets home from school, fill the bathtub with ball pit balls.[3] Pull the shower curtain closed to delay the surprise.

If you are drawing your Ruby's bath water with her in the tub, throw in some colored bath salts or a little safe food coloring. Or scatter soap petals, or flowers. Or bubble bath, if you haven't used it yet. Or a new toy boat. Or foamy soap, shaving cream, or a wind-up toy fish that swims by itself. Epsom salts are fun because they feel cool as they dissolve.[4] Vary the surprises.

Surprise:

If you are packing a quartered apple in your Ben's lunch, put a gummy worm in the center.

Use toys like puppets that can suddenly come to life in your hands. Puppets representing people, dinosaurs, pets, birds, and other animals your child is familiar with can stimulate playful interaction and help develop imaginary play.

---

3   If your child regularly plays in a ball pit you have at home, the balls may get grimy. Just so you know, even a severe hygiene accident can be dealt with by putting the balls loosely into large laundry bags that zip closed, and running them through the washing machine with a disinfectant and very hot water.

4   Ask your doctor whether this extra exposure to magnesium might help April stay calm.

Tip # 4b: Try illusions and magic.

Although your child may have many sensory and developmental struggles, unless he is in the earliest stages of autism he will know full well that dropped objects do not fall up, objects cannot be easily passed through solids, and so on. Truly arresting surprises can be generated for your child by appearing to violate such natural laws. So magic tricks may captivate your ASD child.

Dr. Paul J. Callahan has developed a repertoire of startling magic tricks to increase the focus and attention of the children he works with. He can, as needed, appear to swallow a bone, (AND cough it back up!), pull a pen through one ear to the other, increase interest in small objects by moving and hiding them in a shell game, or making them appear and disappear, and many other alluring tricks requiring dexterity, timing, and imagination.

If you are adept at any tricks, add them to your arsenal of relating to your child with autism.

Books and toys that seem to produce impossible effects are also worth trying.

Example:

George, looking at a picture book about butterflies with his mother, points to the butterflies on each page. Most pages are paper, but the next one is clear plastic. George, unsuspecting, points to the butterfly, and then watches, transfixed, as his mother turns the page and the butterfly appears to fly across the book to the other side. Magic!

Tip # 5: Take advantage of his drive to restore order if your child is difficult to engage.

You can reach your David by creating a mild disorder for him to fix.

Example: Find lost eyeglasses, shoes, or purse.

Suppose your son David has a strong drive to completion and restoring order. You can capitalize on this by removing some item of clothing or an accessory you normally use, whose absence David would notice. You and your spouse, family member, nanny, or helper can misplace certain of those items which your David experiences as a vital part of you. Their absence is the disorder which will beg to be remedied.

Perhaps you misplace your glasses, which you need to read, and David has been helped to spot them prior to your asking for them. "David!" you can exclaim. "Help me! Find my glasses!" Be sure to make the eyeglass sign, circles around your eyes. Sign "find," or "give." David can get them for you right away.

But don't let David off the hook yet. Put your glasses on crooked, or upside down. Push them up on your head like a headband. Try saying and signing "help" again. Even an extremely disordered child will find it hard to resist fixing your glasses. Do you want to try some toy glasses, or plain readers, or sunglasses, on your David? He might be amused.

Similarly, if you happen to "misplace" one of your shoes or slippers in a different part of the room, come loudly clumping up to David with only one on. Where is your other shoe? Can David find it?

For any particular person, simply figure out what items (such as a scarf, a tie, a watch, a purse, or earrings) your child relates to that person, and have him find the items.

If misplacing items is too stressful for your David, start by simply disordering them. Show up with your baseball cap on crooked. If you usually wear a tie, flip it over your shoulder. If you normally wear suspenders, let one of them slip off your shoulder.

Corollary: Your Angela may find your earrings, cuff links, scarf, or watch alien to you and yearn for their removal. Engage her by encouraging her to sign and point "watch off?"

Tip # 6: Stay at your child's eye level or approximate height to maximize interaction.

Remember that it is harder for most people to look up than down.

Tip # 7: If your Alex seems to be lost in space, you can help him orient himself by broadcasting on all channels.

Some remote children with autism seem nearly unreachable, or even seem to be moving further away from you perceptually and cognitively. But you can recapture them. By broadcasting on all channels, we mean that you use all possible means of communication, *not* limited to photos, speaking, signing, strongly expressive gestures, body language, and facial expressions, and you give consistent signals about yourself, like a beacon. Appeal to all the senses your child may find attractive, keeping in mind your own special child's particular sensitivities.

If your Alex is still struggling to make sense out of the enormous sensory storm he lives in, he may need many more clues to orient to you, and he may need great consistency in your appearance for a while. Apparently minor variations may cause Alex to panic or to fail to recognize you. He will be startled if you stop using your signature perfume or aftershave. He may run away screaming if he toddles into your bedroom at night and finds you are wearing white cotton gloves to soften your hands.

If you stop by his school at an odd moment, he might scream on seeing you, or even fail to realize that it is you: you are out of place. He may also find it impossible to accept other people outside of known contexts or outside of familiar places, since they are violating his understanding of the normal order.

We all experience this to some extent. We fail to recognize someone from work when we bump into them in the grocery store, because the context has changed.

During the time that your Alex needs many consistent clues about you, consider using all the time, or part of the time, as appropriate for him or for you, some of the following to get and maintain his attention:

- a characteristic mustache or beard, that you can maintain for a while in the same shape and color

- a signature perfume, cologne, shower gel, or soap

- saturated nail colors, or a different nail polish color on each nail; both the bright color and the variation will attract attention

- distinctive make-up, hair coloring, jewelry, bindi, hair ornament, tie, belt buckle, etc.

- a wrist band with loud bells on it, charm bracelet, ankle bells, lots of jangling and tinkling

- extremely soft textures and bright colors in clothing

- as much physical contact as can be enjoyed

- a lot of talking, singing, humming, and whistling.

Heads-up! Don't think that your nonverbal children with autism do not need to hear language just because they are not speaking yet; they need to be bombarded with it. Repetitive initial sounds in many of the words in a sentence may be helpful, and it is fine if those sentences are on the silly side, such as, "Help Helen hide the haggis." [5]

Just a reminder that if you use a notable scent, accessory, or style of beard, for a long time, your child may identify the smell or accessory as an essential part of your identity. Having identified some of these attributes with you, he may be horrified if you change any of them and may be disoriented sufficiently not to recognize you right away. You will build this needed flexibility over time, with gradual changes and reassurance.

For example, if you know your child with autism identifies your glasses with you, but you must nevertheless get a new eyeglasses prescription, try to get frames closely resembling the previous ones. Introduce them by first showing your child some strongly contrasting glasses on your face, asking him, "These?" Here you are hoping to elicit both communication and assent to the new glasses. If the child shakes his head or says "No" to the grossly contrasting glasses, take those off and replace them with the only slightly different new glasses, and ask, "OK?" or, "Better?" or something similar. [6] This procedure has a good chance of success.

What if your child seems scattered, and is not able to identify objects with you?

---

5   This inspiration for auditory bombardment comes from the work of the eminent speech therapist Lynn Medley, in the US. (Gabriel Garcia Marquez [*Vivir Para Contarla* 2003, p. 472] contributes a Spanish example: *el chocolate del chico de la cachucha chica.*) This technique should work in any language, though for some languages the significant sounds may need to be at the ends of words.

6   Dr. Bruce E. Auerbach worked out this incremental example in real life.

Your Lucy may find it hard to become interested in objects. She may be easily distracted by anything in range, and you may notice that she often looks one way while her hands are busy exploring outside her range of vision.

Check her peripheral vision; she may actually see what she is doing in a wide arc. Many children with autism have wide peripheral vision. But if her hands and eyes simply seem not to work together, you want to help her right away to coordinate them. Start with a simple task with objects she can feel and hear, to make an impression.

Tip # 8: Use sensory-rich, dramatic tasks to strengthen hand-eye coordination.

Have Lucy pick up a wooden block and drop it on a metal pan or cookie sheet to make a thundery noise. If she doesn't seem involved, help her by taking her hand and putting it gently over the block. Narrate and sign "pick up," "drop," or "throw." The sound can help your Lucy realize that SHE did it; her dropping the block on the metal surface created that sound. Have her drop several.

If she is not looking at her hand as she drops blocks, tap her hand or blow on it to see if she can turn toward it and watch what she is doing. You want her to *see* what she is doing, as well as feeling and hearing it. If the sound is too loud for Lucy, drop a towel over the pan to muffle the noise, or fill the pan with water so Lucy hears a splash instead of a crash.

Repeat this dropping blocks a dozen times, or perhaps more, until you see that Lucy is starting to be involved in what she is doing and to feel like continuing. Then start introducing mild disorders: move the pan a bit side to side, or gradually move it away from her. If Lucy becomes distressed, move it back. Check whether Lucy is searching for the pan while you move it around.

Then vary the objects you are using. Try dropping some rubber ducks, polished stones, or plastic fish into the water. Try fizzing bath salts. Continue varying your materials for about 10 or 15 minutes, but stop before Lucy is ready to stop, so that the routine is still attractive to her the next day.

Keep repeating this routine, perhaps using larger or deeper water containers, or louder metal sheets, until your Lucy starts dropping objects into the container or onto the cookie sheet with no prompting or support from you.

Here you have helped Lucy learn how to coordinate her vision with her hands, and you have also let her know first-hand that she can have an effect in the world. This lays the groundwork for Lucy later to understand that her words can have an effect in the world as well.

Tip # 9: Increase your Ava's focus and time on task by selecting furniture that helps define the space around her and adds sensory input.

Furniture shapes and the architecture of the room can contribute considerably to your child's ability to focus and stay with a game, puzzle, or book.

Consider a desk or a table with a deep bay in it that partially surrounds your child when she is sitting. If you have several children on the autism spectrum, a table shaped like an asterisk, with many bays, would be helpful. Half moon and flower shapes could work. Chairs with arms that reach around help define space, as do basket chairs.

You want to take into account relationships among objects in the room and the children's eyes and hands. Scale, shape, and proportion of furniture and objects can help ground each child.

You can also consider meeting sensory needs via the furniture. A yoga ball chair or inflated seat cushion so that your Chandler can bounce a bit as he works on a puzzle may help him concentrate. Some children do well with rocking chairs, or chairs that glide a bit. Some older children with autism may do well with a treadmill or stationary bicycle under the table where they are working.

Tip # 10: Try to minimize distractions in the room where you spend the most time playing and working with your autistic child.

If your Emma is extremely alert and scans the room often, she will be distracted by the sight of other books or toys on the shelves that she is not using at the moment. Try to provide covered storage, with cabinet doors that close, or curtains or blinds, over the materials not in current use. Or store items in plain cardboard boxes.

Depending on what is going on outside, you may need heavy curtains, blinds, or an opaque film on the windows.

Try to avoid fluorescent lighting. It creates sounds and variations in light intensity that can distract children with autism.

Developing coping skills

Tip # 11: To develop coping skills and flexibility, change one small aspect of a predictable routine your child enjoys.

We encourage our children with autism to be able to cope with change by breaking down changes in their environments into the smallest possible units, and then providing many instances for them to practice coping, gradually moving up to increasingly abrupt or complex changes as our children learn to deal with smaller ones.

First, try a small variation to expand an established routine. If your child is throwing beanbags at a target as you hand them to him, move from your accustomed location to a new one. This is a position expansion.

If your child is outdoors pouring sand from a cup into a bucket, move the bucket. This is a location expansion.

If your child easily adjusts to the new location, try several different spots for the bucket.

Try handing your child a soft ball or a squeeze toy to throw at the target instead of a beanbag. This is an object expansion.

If your child handles that change of tossable objects well, have someone else hand him the soft balls. This is a person expansion.

These are all examples of mild disorders you can introduce as expansions in ongoing tasks and play routines. (Dr. Miller used the mnemonic "PLOP" to remind parents and caregivers about types of expansions: *p*erson, *l*ocation, *o*bject, and *p*osition.)

Tip # 12: When your child can accept small changes in predictable routines, try interruptions.

Examples:

Suppose your Noam is pouring small bottles of water into a deep pan. Take a bottle out of his hand just as he is getting ready to pour it.

Suppose your Jacob is blowing bubbles. Just as he takes a deep breath to blow, slip the bubble wand out of his hand.

If your Lucy is able to walk with you, keeping pace with you, and is accustomed to a daily walk, just as you have settled into a comfortable rhythm, turn around and expect her to follow you, saying, "I changed my mind," or "Let's go this way."

When your Anushka is building with blocks, sit down on the floor between her construction site and the pile of blocks, so that she has to get up and walk around you to get another block.

As your children become comfortable with small expansions and larger interruptions, they will be ready to confront dramatic disorder.

Tip # 13: When you think the time is right, try a drastic change in a known environment.

Controlled chaos can be challenging for your child on the autism spectrum, as it is for anyone, but it will stimulate their development. If you think your child is not ready for complete chaos, use a lesser example first and work up.

Create this dramatic disorder in a playroom, outdoors, or anywhere where you have established some set routines and an orderly place for all objects.[7]

Small examples of dramatic change:

Your Riley comes into the dining room and sees that one of the chairs is on the table, seat down, as for floor cleaning. You say, "Oh, no! Riley, let's fix it!" Help him restore the chair to its correct position.

---

7   Your child's bedroom might not be a good choice, especially if your child already has any difficulty going to sleep. (Think about using melatonin to encourage sleep. Ask your doctor.)

Playroom example of large-scale drastic change:

If your Sophie is fortunate enough to have her own space for play, which is used regularly and predictably, with furniture and storage space for toys and art supplies, you can create drastic disorder by overturning the table and chair and scattering toys and drawing materials on the floor, along with a few sheets of wadded-up paper. Have available a wastebasket for the "trash" paper. If your furniture is easy to assemble, you could remove a leg or two. If you have a little rug, you could roll it up. Be sure to create your controlled chaos when Sophie is not present. Don't let her glimpse it before you are ready.

Bring Sophie into the playroom at the usual time, and exclaim, in apparent shock, "Oh my! Look at this mess! We must fix it!" Many children will immediately get to work restoring order. If Sophie showers you with tears instead, help her see that she herself can fix everything, put the dolls back in their house, collect the blocks and put them on the shelf, stack the paper, and gather the crayons into a cup.

It may be easiest to start with the trash.

Outdoor example:

If your Logan enjoys a back yard or garden spot which normally boasts a plastic baby pool, a hose, perhaps a see-saw, or a balance beam, a sand pit and a swing, it too can provide dramatic disorder.

While Logan is at school, turn the baby pool over. If you usually have toys in the baby pool, scatter them in the grass or on the walk. Scatter the sand toys too. Move the garden hose to an unusual spot, tie the swing up, and take the board off of the see-saw. If there is a lawn chair, turn it over. Cover the sand pit with a cloth, or a lid, if it came with one.

When Logan returns, take him outside and say, "Wow! Look at this! Help me fix it!"

Why dramatic disorder is worthwhile:

Coping successfully with chaotic change increases our children's self-confidence and sense of competence. They also benefit from deep pressure which comes from pushing or carrying heavy objects. Their spatial awareness increases as they practice putting away toys. If you work alongside them, you are laying the foundations for cooperative work later with other adults and children.

Why dramatic disorder works:

Using disorder works because it harnesses the powerful drive to create order. While everyone has this drive, it is a turbo-powered motivator for ASD children. Restoring order with their own hands teaches the children that restoration is possible, and that they have some control over it. With practice, our ASD children become increasingly able to tolerate other forms of disorder that characterize our chaotic world. Notice that, to be effective, disorder strategies require your child's previous involvement in the activity or arrangement that you plan to disrupt. You cannot disrupt an unknown routine.

Tip # 14: Remember that dramatic disorder only works if it is a surprise.

Intermezzo

Dramatic disorder in the kitchen

Unless you are adept at some practice of meditative mind and body control, or dehydrated, or wearing adult

Depend® underwear, every now and then you will have to make a pit stop, if only briefly.

But. Things happen while you are not there. Sensory needs can drive your child to create his own dramatic disorder. You'll see.

Example: Kitchen flour bomb.

An eerie stillness has descended over the kitchen, and so has a 10 lb sack of white flour, which appears to have detonated at ceiling height and is still silently filtering through the air.

All the kitchen surfaces from the tops of cabinet doors to the counter to the floor are evenly covered with a soft coating like a new snowfall. The kitchen is peaceful, and, except for the fear of an imminent flour explosion,[8] so are you...

A small trail of white-outlined footprints leads outside, indicating that your child, prudently, has fled.

---

8   Yes, flour dispersed in the air burns explosively.

3

HOW TO MAXIMIZE COMMUNICATION
INDUCE IT!

Children with autism may struggle to communicate, and may live with that frustration and helplessness. But you can relieve it by eliciting communication from your ASD child.

Dr. Miller's method of eliciting communication, *induced communication*, is a routine-based strategy for developing sign, picture, printed, and verbal communication.[1] Your basic communication plan has two parts. One is working with existing routines that your child already knows well, such as scribbling, opening and closing, sending cars down zigzag ramps, putting cups on hooks, or building with blocks. The second part is creating new routines, such as pouring a container of water over a water wheel.

When your child is fully absorbed in her routine, you interrupt the routine, and insist that she communicate before she can return to it. You create communication by interrupting existing systems or—where new routines are concerned—first establishing and then interrupting them.

You see, sabotage always works, and it works across the spectrum. It also works across communication modes, whether

---

1   You may also induce other forms of oral and written communication, via handwriting, keyboarding, or assistive communication.

your child signs, uses picture exchange systems (PECS),[2] a voice output device, or is beginning to talk again. Developing new communication routines to intersperse with established ones is almost always a success for all comers as well. Most of the children in Dr. Miller's practice over the years were nonverbal or beginners at talking, and so his tips are oriented to that population. But his methods of routine interruption/ sabotage, and offering new routines for communication, can be used productively in all communication modes, for all children with autism.

Let's get started using induced communication to teach our children signs, pictures, spoken, and printed words!

Communication

Tip # 15: Hand signing is essential.

We cannot overstate the power of signing for your nonverbal or not yet fully verbal child with autism. Signing increases your child's awareness of spoken language, increases the number of words he recognizes when they are spoken (receptive language), and increases his ability to express himself. And even for typical children, signing increases IQ.

Some parents fear that signing will slow the development of speech, but all our experience points to just the opposite: when you speak *and* sign, signing clarifies meaning and can help induce speech.

---

2   Especially for children with autism who are just developing their full body awareness, PECS with abstract symbols may not be an ideal choice for the first, early communication system. PECS are remote from the body, give virtually no sensory feedback, and so may be aggravating, distracting, and alien, particularly when accompanied by apparently unrelated and unrecognized oral reinforcers. Signing is a better first choice for many sensory-needy ASD children to begin with. Interesting, significant photos and realistic pictures are an important adjunct for later communication.

Tip # 16: Yes! Some nonverbal kids with autism become able to speak when they sign. In such cases signing overcomes the child's apraxia of speech.

Example:

George's father brings him French fries to add to his lunch at school. As George watches, mouth watering, his father says and signs, "French fries," and does not offer any to George until George signs, "Give" to request them. George takes a few and begins munching them, with obvious enjoyment. Imagine the father's surprise when Connor, a previously nonverbal classmate, signs, "Give" too, and simultaneously pipes up in his six-year-old voice, "*Gih*"!

Connor's teacher discovered that he had a vocabulary of expressive language, words he could actually SAY, with practice, if he signed them.

To sum up:

- Signing increases IQ.
- Signing helps build receptive and expressive vocabulary.
- Signing can stimulate speech and reduce or bypass apraxia.
- Signing can reduce frustration.

Tip # 17: Make signing interesting, fun, meaningful, emotional, and as graphic as possible.

This means that signs should be used for basic survival communication at first, and adults should use signs with each other as well as with the child who has autism. They should seem to enjoy signing. Your child may especially appreciate verbs, such as "jump,"[3] but highly valued nouns have an important place too.

Make your signs strongly descriptive. Make your signs graphic and fun! Add meaning with body language, facial expression, the angle of your head, mime, eye contact, and even size of the sign.

Examples:

If you are signing "crazy" by making a circle at your temple with your index finger, it adds to the craziness to cross your eyes, or wiggle your head, or stick out your tongue.[4]

Tip # 18: Don't forget to talk while you are signing.

This may mean that you want to use a signing method that follows the word order of normal speech, such as signed Exact English. Consult your speech therapist. If your child already has a good grasp of some spoken language, at first you can model your speech on your child's usual speech pattern. If your Lakshmi typically speaks in two- or three-word sentences, you should too. Long sentences with subjunctive clauses will not help at this stage.

The power of narration to increase your child's receptive vocabulary and increase his language competence is enormous. So as you go through the day, narrate: describe what your child is doing, and what you are doing, in simple, direct language. Comment on the weather, or anything else compelling that you can point to and share an interest in.

---

3   Our Ben appreciated making the "jump" sign with vigor. He once invited a fully-clothed janitor to jump into the hotel pool with us, in midwinter, with his coat on. Ben's sign was so persuasive that the janitor apologized for declining Ben's invitation.

4   Stacy Fiske showed us this multi-dimensional example.

Try not to bounce your hands as you sign; bouncing signs are hard to track.

Tip # 19: Select or adapt the signs you use to your child's current condition.

Suppose, for example, that your Joshua does not have enough body awareness just yet to make a conventional "drink" sign away from his mouth. Choose signs for him that give him skin contact. You can substitute signing "drink" by having him trace lightly down his throat with his index finger.

Why this works:

Some children with autism have so little sensation or body awareness, so little physical sense that they exist, that they cannot sign in the air because they do not feel the finger motion sufficiently. Those kids may need to rely, at least at first, on signs that increase sensory input because they touch the body or make noise. You may need to adapt your child's signs to his current neurological state.

Suppose your Roberto loves his dog but cannot make the conventional sign for "dog," snapping his fingers and then slapping his thigh as if calling the dog. The Miller "dog" sign might be right for him. Have Roberto hold his two hands up in front of his chest with the wrists bent down like paws, and ask him to open his mouth to pant. If he is able, he can let his tongue loll out. This Miller dog sign is graphic, immediately recognizable, and fun for most kids to do.

Parents should note that you can teach your dog to respond to signed commands as well, so that even your nonverbal ASD child can still communicate with his dog.

Tip # 20: Adapt your sign teaching to your own child's sensitivities and neurological state.

Use hand-over-hand instruction for children who can tolerate that much touch; for others, sign while standing or kneeling beside your child, parallel to his signing.

You may need to select child-specific signs, provide sensory input while you are teaching, and be sure to try to establish the new sign in context.

Your Chloe may really appreciate skin contact, and can quickly be taught new signs by hand-over-hand instruction, in which you hold her hands to help her make the signs. But your Liam may be so overwhelmed by skin contact, so flooded with sensation, that he cannot learn anything hand-over-hand. In his case stand or sit beside him, parallel, and sign beside him. Try not to raise your hands too high; it is easier to look down than up.

If your Emily seems unable to sign in either case, she may need more stimulation of her hands, and some exercises showing her how to use her hands.

Example: Developing a "come" sign for Emily.
PROBLEM:

Emily may be experiencing a common problem in trying to learn that the "come" sign will bring someone closer. Why should the movements of her hand as she brings it against her chest be influential in bringing someone closer? Parents speculate that their children may even find the "come" sign counterintuitive, since the motion of hands curling in toward themselves is the exact opposite of throwing their arms up and open, a gesture they may have used since infancy to request that someone come and pick them up.

PROCEDURE:

Emily loved pouring water over a water wheel in a dishpan. Consequently, to use the power of that routine to motivate Emily to sign, her mother, standing across the room from Emily and her toys, held out a bottle of water, to encourage Emily to make the "come" sign. Emily's father worked behind his daughter, hand-over-hand, to model the sign.

RESPONSE:

On the first try, Emily, seeing the water bottle her mother was holding, not unreasonably signed "more," which had served her well in the past. When "more" did not work, Emily began to try to use her father's hands to sign.

PROVIDE MORE SENSORY INPUT.

Since Emily did not use her own hands to sign, Dr. Miller would suggest that she may not have enough sensation in her hands, or might lack a fully developed sense of how her hands work. (Of course, she might just enjoy making Daddy sign.)

If you suspect that your child, like Emily, needs more feeling in her hands, and more practice using them, you can set up a situation in which your child receives some deep pressure and also some stimulation for her hands. The deep pressure will help her focus, and the exercises will make her more aware of her hands.

One way to supply this deep pressure and hand exercise is to have your Emily lie down on the floor, and carefully place one or two moderately heavy objects on her. You could use old telephone books, a dictionary, a large floor pillow, a large bag of rice, or anything safe with rounded contours. Try different placements; over a large bone may be helpful.

As soon as she feels the books or other items weighing her down, show Emily how to push them off, first with the right hand, then with the left hand. Sometimes, hold one of her hands so that she has to use the opposite hand and cross the midline of her body.[5] After about five minutes of varying pressures, return to teaching the "come" sign.

After a little exercise, almost immediately after her mother held out the bottle of water, Emily eagerly put out a hand and moved it decisively toward her chest with the clear expectation that this movement would bring her mother (and the bottle) a step closer. She got the point!

Your Emily will be delighted to succeed in bringing people closer with her new "come" sign.

In general, you want to remember to use deep pressure to stimulate hand signing. If you think that lack of hand awareness may be the reason behind your child's inability to make new signs, we recommend that you try pressure-generating options like the ones suggested for Emily above. You can also try games and exercises which strengthen the hands, such as squeezing soft balls, and exercises which increase body awareness in general, such as tug of war with a rope.

Deep pressure and rough and tumble may help relieve apraxia too.

Tip # 21: Take advantage of natural opportunities to teach new signs.

Since Emily in the previous case was accustomed to the feel of her hands pouring water, after a pouring session would be a productive time to teach the "pour" sign.

If you are driving by a particularly ripe barnyard on a car trip, you can teach the "stink" sign.

---

5   Crossing midline stimulates the corpus callosum.

If your toddler is captivated by the sound of coughing, you can teach him to sign "more," and then cough on command. He will learn the "more" sign on the spot. In a few minutes you will have a natural opportunity to teach "enough," or "all finished."

Tip # 22: Evoke signs that are latent in your child by capturing natural gestures.

Your Kira may have an urgent wish to communicate, but still face formidable obstacles to initiating communication. You can help her by evoking signs that have not yet fully appeared.

To induce sign communication, involve your Kira in some favorite activity such as pouring water into a large basin. Have at hand many of the containers of water she usually uses. Keep handing them to her and saying, "Pour!" until she becomes totally dedicated to pouring on her own. This degree of absorption tells you that Kira now has a water pouring routine that she needs and wants to maintain.

When you see that your Kira is fully engaged in her pouring routine, interrupt her pouring by taking the bottle from her hand just as she is tilting it. Kira, needing to maintain her pouring routine, may well make a small or inadvertent pouring motion as if the bottle were still in her hand.

If you see this motion, react immediately by returning the bottle to her *as if* her motion were a true expression of her intent. Here, you say, "Oh, Kira wants to pour." With repetition, her pouring gesture becomes a symbol as she begins to expect the bottle back each time she makes that particular gesture. Over time you can shape the gesture into a recognizable sign, if it isn't already.

To add more functional signs to your child's signing vocabulary, develop his existing play routines to capture the natural gestures in the routines. You can also add new routines which can be interrupted to capture their natural gestures.

In each case, you are using the Miller strategy for eliciting and inducing signing. Parents, relatives, and other carers are, in effect, creating motivation within their children to use signing in everyday life, to gain objects the children want to restore their interrupted routines. Over time, this ability to make a few signs can be expanded to make more complicated requests, begin to develop conversations, and increase your child's pleasure in communicating.

Tip # 23: Don't forget to generalize the sign.

If "come" is a new sign for Eva, when we teach it we want to make it clear that its meaning is not dependent on who makes the sign, who sees it, or their location. So use your new signs with different people and from different locations, in varying contexts. Use the "pour" sign at the table, in the bathtub, over the sink, and at the pool.

Tip # 24: Don't forget to sign to other adults in your child's presence.

The more signing your children see, the more proficient they will become. Also they can see that signing is not a punishment, or only a baby thing to do: it has prestige.

Tip # 25: What to do if your child uses one sign for everything?

Perhaps your Sue Ann only knows the "more" sign, and tries to make it contain entire universes. Don't yield to the natural temptation to accommodate Sue Ann's desire to sign "more" in every context, even though you may know what she means. Part of her autism may be the struggle to expand communication. But you want Sue Ann to communicate fully.

Acknowledge her "more" sign, but help her expand what she signs. You can request specifics. "More spinach?" you can ask, "or more ice cream?" "More celery, or a Dove bar?"

If Sue Ann does not already nod her head yes and shake her head no, help her do this in context by offering preferred toys and then adding to her awareness of her face and head by touching under her chin with a slight upward pressure to help her start nodding yes, or slight pressure around the ear to help her shake her head no. (Consult your speech therapist for techniques.) Nodding yes, shaking your head no, blowing kisses, and making thumbs up signs are some of the easier early communicative gestures you can add to diversify your child's communication.

Tip # 26: Help your child develop a repertoire of signing conversations that are routine for him.

Don't forget that your child with autism may find comfort and predictability in routines. You can use this power to help foster fluency in signing by teaching, according to your child's personal interests, little conversations which have a small number of variations and which have a predictable outcome. These can become signing routines, which he will be happy to enjoy with you, and to expand. You can build his signing repertoire by increasing the number of these little conversations, which over time can add up to a considerable store of communication to use with everyone.

At first you may use minimal language. Still, speak as you sign. Here is an example of a set conversation one parent used for a young child who loved babies:

Your Joel signs: "Look, baby."

You reply: "Oh! Pretty baby."

Joel asks: "Joel hold baby?"

You say: "OK. Sit down, hold baby."

Joel notes: "Baby beautiful."

You agree: "Yes. Kiss baby?"

Joel: "Yes."

If your child has an attitude about your appearance, you may be able to use that attitude to motivate him to carry out an entire conversation. You can expand and sabotage it from time to time. One mother discovered that her son despised barrettes in her hair, and also preferred that she not wear earrings or watches. The ticking sound of her reliable waterproof Timex seemed to irritate him. He had flushed several, yet somehow she still seemed to have one on her wrist!

Your Alex points and signs: "Watch off!"

You reply: "Alex wants Mom's watch off?"

Alex nods vigorously: "Yes!"

Here you can try a diversion.

You say and sign: "Watch loud?"

Alex signs: "Yes. Off!"

You say: "OK."

But you don't DO anything, which can prompt Alex to sign again:

Alex: "Off!"

You agree again, but expand: "OK. Now or later?"

Alex: "Now!"

You slowly remove the watch: "Put in pocket?"

Alex: "Yes." Points at earrings, signs, "Off."

Still working it, you sign: "Alex wants Mom's earrings off?"

Alex: "Yes!"

You reply: "Oh. One earring or two earrings?"

Alex: "Two!" etc.

You may justifiably feel that your child has no business telling you how to dress and accessorize. But our first priority here is to get communication going.

You can expand and prolong these conversations for as long as your child can cope. He will enjoy the power he has to cause change in the world.

If your imaginative and persistent attempts to teach signing are stalling out, you may need to drop back one step. Your child may not be able to hear words as separate meaningful elements of sound.

What if your child seems not to hear words as separate, significant sounds?

If your Latisha seems not to respond when you call her name, and does not come when you call, of course you will have her hearing tested. And you will consult your speech therapist. But if Latisha has normal hearing and still is not responding, the issue may be that she does not distinguish words from other sounds in the environment: lawn mowers, street vendors, traffic sounds, airplane roaring overhead, or birds singing. Dr. Miller suggests the following steps to embed words in physical actions so that words begin to have meaning for your child. That embedding process will help teach your child to hear and respond to you.

A fun and playful method of overcoming word deafness in children with autism

1. Find an activity your child is drawn to, such as climbing up and sliding down a playground slide, or playing with you on a see-saw.

2. Have your Latisha complete the entire routine, helping her if she needs help, as you narrate each step in the routine, giving the appropriate language to her. You can say and sign "Climb," "Up," "Sit down," "Down," "Slide," "Get up," "Come," and "Stop." For the see-saw you could say and sign "Sit down," "Up," "Down," and "Get up."

3. Try to be sure Latisha sees your signs as she is carrying out the action you refer to. You want to pair the word, in both signed and spoken form, with the action it represents. If you have a choice of signs in the system you are using, choose the one that most closely resembles the action that it stands for.

4. Don't forget to speak as you sign: you want Latisha to hear you!

5. Watch for some indication that Latisha is waiting for the manual sign and spoken word before proceeding. If you don't see this hesitation, interrupt her at a dramatic point, such as just as she is getting ready to slip down the slide, and say and sign "DOWN!" dramatically. Then let her slide down. You can try this interrupting and sabotaging trick at other points as well.

6. Use the signs and words Latisha is familiar with from the slide with different people, so she knows that

the signs and words apply to everyone. You can try illustrating this at home with a toy slide and a doll.

7. Then, use these signs and spoken words in many different situations so that Latisha knows they apply not only at the playground by the slide, but everywhere.

Inducing communication with photographs

The next step you need to take in communicating with your ASD child is to establish that photos represent real things. This step generates basic symbolic representation for your child, a key to abstract communicating.

To induce communication with pictures, you use a strategy like the one for inducing signs. Let's say your Noah enjoys a routine coloring with crayons. This time, while Noah is scribbling, you "steal" Noah's crayon and then present him with several pictures, one of which is a photo of the crayon Noah needs to continue his scribbling routine. Once Noah selects the correct picture and hands it to you, you narrate, "Noah wants the crayon," and as you say so, you give the crayon back to Noah.

Your Noah will learn to use other pictures to get objects he needs to continue several of his other favorite routines. Don't be discouraged if this takes several attempts to get started. Induced picture communication may be more challenging than signs for many children with autism because it requires the child eventually to notice differences among several pictures to find the exact one that communicates his need for a particular object.

Tip # 27: To show your child that photos can stand for real things, interrupt an ongoing routine your child is absorbed in and remove an object your child needs, replacing it with a photo.

Return the desired object only when your child offers the photo in exchange. You may need to prompt him for a while.

Another way to illustrate for your Harry that photographs represent real things is to make several cards with part of an object on one side, and a photograph or clear drawing of the same object on the other side. You might try cutting a half-inch slice vertically off a cardboard juice box, mounting it on one side of a card, and on the other, glue a photo or a downloaded image from the web of the same juice box. Flip the card from the object to the picture side several times where your Harry can see it. About half of a disposable cup mounted on one side of a card, with a photo of the cup on the other, is another possibility. A plastic spoon, a slice of a vitamin bottle, or part of a small toy; you will think of many other examples.

Example:

You can develop picture-object relations with your Harry so that Harry knows photos are meaningful symbols, by requiring that he exchange the photo for the missing item.

First, choose some objects that Harry uses in some of the play routines he enjoys, such as painting, zipping a toy car down a ramp, hanging cups on cupboard hooks, or hammering balls into a toy bench or down a chute.

Make clear photos of the paintbrush, toy car, cup, toy hammer, and ball.[6] Preferably, these photos should show the objects on a plain background, with no other distractions. At this stage the photos should be of the identical objects he normally uses in his routines, not just any toy car, but the one (or one of the ones) he sends down the ramp, etc.

You want to convey the idea that the photo can serve as a request for the item. Here is one way to get that notion across:

Place the picture of the paintbrush next to Harry while he is using the brush for painting. When the opportunity arises, "steal" his brush. When he looks for the brush, point to the photo. If he gives you the photo, say, "Harry wants the paintbrush," take the photo, and return the brush immediately.

Harry will soon see that he can get his brush back by giving you the picture of the brush in exchange.

Other examples:

Try several repetitions and variations. Place a picture of the toy car next to Harry while he is sending cars down the zigzag ramp. Then, "steal" his car. Wait for him to offer you the photo of the toy car, saying, "Harry wants the car." If he does not hand the photo to you, point to it. When you take the photo from him, instantly return the car. In this case Harry sees that to get his car back, he has to first give you the picture of a car.

If your Harry likes to hang cups on cup hooks, have a picture of a cup next to Harry while he is engaged in his routine of hanging cups up. Then, steal the last cup: do not

---

6   Some children may be advanced enough to recognize line drawings, or colorful paintings, which are more abstract as representations of objects, but photos are most helpful to start. The Richard Scarry drawings and books work for some children, because they are not too exaggerated and they are outlined in black for high contrast.

let him put the last cup on the hook until he gives you the picture of the cup. He may be highly motivated to get the last cup because of his urge for completion, so this is a productive moment for communication. You might try to capture that notion by signing and saying, "Harry wants to finish the cups."

Set up the toy workbench with the hammer and colored balls that Harry uses in one of his routines, to hammer the balls into holes one after another. Put a photo of the toy hammer next to the toy workbench, and then "steal" his hammer. Harry must give you the photo of the toy hammer to get the hammer back, so he can continue the routine. You can, for some children, take this opportunity to teach a "give" sign, such as the graphic one used by Dr. Miller, slapping one flat open palm with the palm of the other hand.

Put a photo of the colored balls next to the toy workbench, and let Harry start hammering a ball into the bench. Then interrupt him by stealing all the other balls. Wait for him to give you the corresponding photo. If he does not, point to it and/or sign "give." He gets the remaining balls back only when he gives you the photo of them. Remember to narrate.

Tip # 28: Now, offer two different photos to teach your child to discriminate between them.

Since Harry now knows pictures represent real things, and can serve as requests for these things, you can teach him to look at photos more closely, to give you a specific picture to get just the object he wants.

Repeat some of the routines mentioned earlier, except that this time you place two contrasting pictures next to your Harry. For example, while he is painting, place the photo of the brush alongside the photo of a cup. Opportunely, take his paintbrush. To get the brush back, your Harry should give you the photo of the brush. Check to see that he is looking at both photos before he chooses one. Switch locations of the brush and cup or other photos from time to time to make certain your Harry is not simply picking up the photo he finds in a particular spot.

Next, alongside the car-down-the-ramp toy, put down two different photos, one of a toy car and another of a different toy, such as the hammer, for Harry to choose from. Try to watch his eyes so you can be sure he is looking at both photographs. Change positions of the photos from time to time to make certain Harry is identifying the correct photo and not responding to location.

Another example: while Harry is putting his set of cups on hooks, place two photos next to him, one of a cup and another of a ball. Before he hangs up the last cup, steal the cup away. Again, Harry needs to pick the right photo to get the cup you have stolen. Shift locations of the pictures so that Harry doesn't confuse the location of the photo with the meaning of the image on it.

Then, while Harry is hammering toy balls into the toy bench, a routine he enjoys and knows well, place photos of a hammer and a cup next to him. After you steal the toy hammer, Harry should offer you the photo of the hammer to get it back. Switch locations of photos from time to time. Continue to narrate.

Tip # 29a: When you are offering your child a choice, try not to give away the answer you are seeking by pointing or staring at the correct photo! Your child may read your body language very well for clues.

Tip # 29b: When you, on the contrary, are teaching your child to follow your gaze, you must stare at your preferred choice!

Once your Harry is clearly looking at the photos and can dependably pick the desired item's photo, you can increase his versatility and scanning ability by offering three photos, or more.

Now that you have shown Harry that pictures can represent real objects, you can show him that pictures can also depict actions and give instructions. (Yes, here we are building awareness of nouns and verbs.) When you show photos giving instructions, you increase your child's understanding of symbols. By extracting more meaning from photographs, you are showing that photos can represent actions and sequences, too.

Tip # 30a: Use photograph sequences to give instructions.

If your Ben is strongly driven to restore order, fix broken items, or complete routines, you can teach him to understand instructions via photos.

First, get a set of clear pictures of your Ben fixing something broken, restoring order, or finishing different routines that he cares about. Adapt these to your child's changing interests. Here are some possibilities:

1. Picking up a capsized table. Show Ben in two photos: in one, standing in front of the capsized table; in the other, setting it upright.

2. Building a tower with boards or blocks. Again, make two pictures: one with Ben standing in front of the tower boards; in the other, stacking a board in its proper position. It might make sense to have a tower

partially built, so that the purpose is clear in the second photo.

3. Instead of small or light-weight blocks, you may find that your larger, stronger or older autistic child finds it interesting to work with longer boards that are more convenient for them to grasp, cut off in approximately18-inch lengths. If you sand these, and use an indelible marker or a lumber crayon to mark off the ends to show your child how to stack them in a square, he may participate enthusiastically. You can modify these boards with velcro strips on the ends for construction, or by drilling shallow holes that will accommodate dowel rods for tinker toy type expansions of play. You may capture your younger or highly visually motivated youngster with autism if you offer bright colored textured blocks such as bristle blocks.

4. Picking up trash and putting it in a wastebasket. Again you want to show Ben in two pictures in sequence; first he should be picking up a piece of paper in front of the wastebasket; in the second he should be dropping it into the wastebasket.

5. Bouncing on a trampoline. Use two pictures; one should show Ben standing in front of the trampoline; in the other he should be enthusiastically bouncing on it.

6. Working a puzzle. For this example, Ben should be photographed holding a puzzle piece and then putting it in its proper place. You may get the strongest response in this example and similar ones that have a clear completion point if you photograph the *last* puzzle piece going in.

Then, after preparing these different situations (e.g. the table overturned, a puzzle on the table, some trash on the floor near the wastebasket, a partially constructed tower with more boards handy), or others appropriate for your child, show Ben the first photo from one of the sequences. At first, you may need to guide him to what the photo represents.

If you show the picture of him standing by the overturned table, he may at first need to be led to the capsized table. Then show him the second photo. If he does not turn the table upright then, point to the picture and help him right the table. It will probably take him a few tries before he understands that the pictures tell him what to do. Practice, practice, practice!

Tip # 30b: Use a photo schedule to show your Thomas what to expect each day.

Make clear color photos of each central event in Thomas' day, and arrange them in order somewhere convenient for him to see, on a portable strip of velcro-faced cardboard, on your front door, or wherever works best for you. Try to put it at his eye level if it is not portable. Make an effort to guess which are the most important events to your Thomas. He may expect the school bus ride, but he may also expect the route to go by the fire station, so the landmarks along the way may be helpful for him to see, too.

Since you want to start accustoming your Thomas to look at images in the same way as he would read, arrange your photos in the order that your printed language reads, when possible.

If Thomas wants to rearrange the photos and use them to communicate with you, excellent! Make him

a large assortment. Narrate what is going to happen during the day in the correct sequence, anyway, even as he is taking the photos down.

Some children will not know that the photos showing a school bus, lunch, the playground, the bus, landmarks, and home again refer to them. At first, you may need to use photos of your Thomas on the bus, in the school lunchroom, and in all the relevant places for him to understand that the photo schedule applies to him.

About acquiring spoken language

We do not need to tell you that if your child never spoke, or lost language when he acquired autism, you child needs a skilled speech therapist with a record of success.

Find that therapist. Be persistent. Your child can learn to talk again at any age.

Even if you are not a speech therapist yourself, you can help your nonverbal child begin to regain speech.

Tip # 31: Treat all communication attempts as meaningful.

If your nonverbal child attempts to speak, repeat his sounds and acknowledge them. Work them into the conversation so that he knows he was heard and appreciated, even if not fully understood. Try to use words which begin with the sounds he made. Pay attention to him when he vocalizes. Never tease him about his sounds, and never dampen them. Encourage all vocalizing, no matter how loud, indiscriminate, or poorly timed.

Tip # 32: Don't prompt with a
vague, "Use your words."

This does not help, for some of the same reasons that "Good
job" is not productive. It produces another conglomeration
of sound that your child needs to try to decipher at the same
time as he is trying to plan how to use his throat and mouth
to shape a word. And, "Use your words" can be hard to
interpret, since it is not concrete, like, "BANG! The balloon
burst!" The main message your child is likely to receive is that
he is already failing.

Tip # 33: Unless your child is highly
verbal, try to avoid questions when
talking to your autistic child.

When you are talking to your child with autism, remember
that it may be much easier for him to complete an interrupted
sentence, with a sign or a word, than it is to answer a question.

Often words like "who," "what," "where," "when," "why,"
and "which one" may have little meaning to your child with
autism. They may also be inhibited from answering direct
questions because of fear of making a mistake.

If your Tyrell does not complete the sentence you left
dangling for him, you finish it yourself, speaking and signing.
If Tyrell did finish your sentence for you, but only signed,
you say what he signed; if he spoke, you supply the sign.

What if your verbal child is echolalic? Grounded verbal communication.

Your Brodie may be able to speak well, and fluently, but
sometimes he seems unaware of the meaning of what he
is saying. He may be able to repeat entire newscasts, TV

commercials, and popular songs, but does not seem to know what they convey.

Tip # 34a: You can use induced communication to ground your Brodie's language.

Your goal here is to embed the words that Brodie knows into routines that work for him, so that the words acquire a concrete meaning. You can start very simply.

As before, when helping children communicate by inducing signs, when you teach your Brodie to fill his words with meaning, you involve him in a pleasant routine, and then interrupt it.

Maybe Brodie likes to buzz his toy airplanes around in the air and then taxi them into a parking position on a toy runway.

Hand him a few toy airplanes, and as he gets absorbed in flying and landing them, take away the remaining toy planes. As Brodie reaches for another, you say, "Plane." If Brodie also says, "Plane," give it to him. Repeat often. Then try holding out another plane without saying anything.

When Brodie says, "Plane" to request one, without a prompt from you, you know that the word has meaning for him in context.

Tip # 34b: As with newly established signs, don't forget to generalize Brodie's newly meaningful words.

Now you are sure Brodie knows his toy planes are planes. When you are outside and one roars by overhead, point to it and see if Brodie will identify it as a plane, too. If not, you say, "Plane." Take every opportunity to point out planes on the TV, in books and magazines, and in real life. Work at it. Think about driving to the airport to show some real ones.[7]

Reciprocal communication

To make communication truly fruitful, you want your autistic child to be able to reciprocate. But reciprocity may be difficult to induce. Here is one way to start.

Tip # 35: Create reciprocity by enabling your child to respond to an adult's request, and make requests of his own.

Some physical props will help. Plan on sitting your Ryan at one end of a long table, with a puzzle frame and a box full of pegboard pegs. At the other end, you sit with a pegboard and the puzzle pieces that Ryan needs.

You are going to be communicating about your mutual needs. But first, consider several ways to make the necessary interchange of puzzle pieces and pegs interesting and dynamic. That way you show how fun it can be to interact with people.

Dr. Miller had a carpenter construct a small-scale wooden bridge for this purpose. You can make one to any suitable dimensions, but a guardrail is a good idea. Dr. Miller's was mostly yellow with dark blue trim, colors which help with visual acuity for children with autism. The bridge is useful for some of the same reasons that the Elevated Square is useful; it limits the options for what to do with the puzzle pieces and pegs, and it sends them in the right direction each time. And it is fun: Ryan can roll a peg across the bridge to you, and you can shoot a puzzle piece back.

---

7   Yes, we did this. More than once.

A small toy wagon to push and pull back and forth is another good option.

Another way to make reciprocity fun is to find a mobile toy you can send back and forth to each other. This toy should be appealing but work in a simple, direct way so as to involve your Ryan without discouraging him. A brightly-colored toy pickup truck that can hold the pegs and puzzle pieces would be a good choice. A friction-powered race car might work, or a toy mail truck whose doors open. Use a rubber band to keep the items secure if needed. Wind-up vehicles may be too complicated: judge your own child's ability to deal with frustration. (Some simple spring-loaded toys such as Tomy's green dragon on wheels go when you push down on the head.) You can run these vehicles on the table top or on the bridge.

Now sit down with the wooden bridge between you. You clearly have what Ryan needs, and Ryan has what you need.

In the next step, send Ryan a photo of a peg. Ryan, by return toy pickup truck across the bridge, can send you a peg.

With someone else's help as needed, help Ryan send you a picture of a puzzle piece. You then respond with the actual puzzle piece. Narrate, "Oh, Ryan needs a piece of his puzzle."

With the need established, you can continue to exchange pegs and puzzle pieces. Stop while Ryan is still interested.

Don't be satisfied with photo communication reciprocity; try signs, printed words, and, to the extent that your child is able to speak, spoken words.

Next time, you can use this same exchange procedure, offering printed words on cards instead of photos, if your Ryan is learning to read. Another time you can use signs, narrating while you are signing, and of course, if your Ryan is verbal, speak.

Variation on establishing reciprocity: how to get Ben to respond to your requests

Your Ben may already respond beautifully to the notion of exchanging puzzle pieces with you directly, when you have the puzzle pieces he needs to complete his puzzle and he has puzzle pieces you need to complete your puzzle. He knows that he has to give you a puzzle piece from his side before you will give him one from your side.

You can build on that exchange pattern to make it more communicative in the following manner. Suppose you are both at a table facing each other. Ben has a puzzle, but instead of a puzzle you have two jars in front of you. Both have lids with openings cut in them. One jar lid has a small square hole in it to allow dice to fall through; the other jar has a slot cut in it to allow small metal discs such as those on the ends of frozen orange juice cans to drop through. You have a dozen or so dice and metal discs, and you also have a photo or a clear drawing of the disc and of a die. If you don't have time or the equipment to photograph or Xerox® the objects, simply draw them on separate cards (dice, disc, puzzle piece).

Then, put the puzzle pieces on your side and the disc and dice on Ben's side. Ben also has pictures of puzzle pieces on his side.

First, Ben starts filling in his puzzle with the pieces available to him on his side of the table. Then, he runs out of puzzle pieces while there are still a number of spaces to fill. While this is going on, you are happily dropping discs and dies into their respective bottles until you run out of discs and dice.

Now you have a request that you want to make. Ben and you now exchange pictures. He gives you a picture of a puzzle piece while you give him a picture of a disc. You hold the puzzle piece in your hand so he can see it. Then, you point to the picture of the disc. He responds to the picture of a disc by picking up the disc, not a die. As he gives you the disc, you give him the puzzle piece.

Try to do this at the same time. Then, what previously was just a simple exchange now becomes an exchange dictated by the pictures each of you exchange to indicate the object you need. You have each made a request, and had it granted.

Once this request-making pattern is established, complicate the set-up by having Ben choose the disc or dice photo from among a variety of other pictures.

Another variation would be for him to get the objects you need when they are located a few feet from the table.

Yet another variation, with a change of materials, could happen in the kitchen. Suppose you are beating up eggs for an omelet and you "lose" the fork... You give Ben a picture of the fork, to request him to bring one to you so you can continue beating up the eggs.

Tip # 36: Help your Ryan learn to read using induced printed word communication.

The next step, a huge one for many children with autism, is to introduce printed word communication. This strategy follows the same form as picture communication. The difference is that instead of photographs, you substitute printed words.

While you can make your own printed word cards on a computer, or hand-letter them on 3 × 5 inch cards and other materials, you could also consider using the vocabulary and materials from the Symbol Accentuation Reading Program (SARP). The advantage of using Dr. Miller's SARP program is that the cards in that series convey meaning directly, rather than by associating the printed word with a picture. Instead, the SARP cards show a drawing which morphs partly into the word itself on the card. This pictorial method of laying the groundwork for reading by picture-word fusion can convey the meaning of the word readily, gradually moving to the conventionally printed word alone.[8]

Vivid words in the SARP which are particularly appropriate to start with might be bird, cat, mop, rat, walk, car, candy, toilet, and shower. But be guided by what motivates your own youngster.

Then, as before with picture communication, interrupt a routine your child enjoys, and request communication to continue it. For example, when your Ryan has immersed himself in a routine of placing cups on hooks, you steal the cup he needs to complete the routine. Ryan can get the cup back only when he offers you the printed word "cup," which he must pick from among other words. Similarly, when Ryan is engaged with sending a car down his zigzag ramp, and the caregiver takes the car, Ryan must select the word "car" from among several other words and offer it in exchange to the caregiver to get the car and continue sending it down the ramp.

If you child is in school, talk to his teachers about using morphing technologies to teach sight words. The school staff may include an electronic media specialist who would be able to create morphed materials for you.

Tip # 37: Add meaning and excitement to reading by dramatizing words.

Choose some exciting verbs. "Jump" and "fall" are excellent examples. Then get some large photos of your Adrian, full face, profile, and partly turned, if you can.

---

8   This method is evidence-based; see for example Kieron Sheehy (2005) "Morphing images: a potential tool for teaching word recognition to children with severe learning difficulties." *British Journal of Educational Technology 36*, 2, 292–301.

Familiarize Adrian with the words "jump" and "fall," if possible using morphing illustrations like those from Symbol Accentuation. Have Adrian jump or fall each time he sees one of these words on the monitor, on your computer, or on a piece of paper.

Then show Adrian the accentuated form of the words, which still have some morphed characteristics (these would be the second card in the SARP flashcard set).

Does he jump, or fall down?

Now show Adrian the three views of himself. Have him touch the photos, while you say his name each time.

Take Adrian's pictures and place them above the accentuated word "jump" on an easel, or any other surface that works for you. Again help him point to himself in each photo, and say his name each time. Then point to the word "jump," and say it.

Now both together: "Adrian, jump!"

If he doesn't, help him do it. Try again. Then simply point to the photos and to the word.

When Adrian jumps when you point to his photos and the printed word "jump," he is on the way to reading comprehension! Set up "Adrian falls!" the same way.

In general, you want to be sure that in all reading, as your Cyril acquires new words, he applies them immediately so that he retains the meaning. For example, if you teach Cyril the word "sip," immediately take a little drink yourself, and have him do so as well. If you teach the word "rip," immediately tear a piece of paper in two, and have him do the same.

Induced communication leading to writing

Tip # 38: At first, you might try setting up writing equipment that gives a lot of body awareness information to your Yasmin as she writes.

Example:

Instead of using a large pad of soft paper with lines, and a large soft dark-leaded pencil or crayon, roll out a layer of modeling clay in a cookie sheet and give your child a stylus or a pencil to write with.

Your Yasmin can trace along the edge of a ruler in the clay for a straight line, around a small plate for a circle.

Other ways to increase sensory feedback to make writing easier include: using a pencil with a fuzzy coating or a squeezable surface; writing on fine sandpaper; using a battery-powered pen that vibrates; using a musical writing pad that plays jazzy music as long as the pen is in contact with the surface. Parents note that you can also try toys that help make writing fun and increase the sensory feedback from making letters and numbers, such as the Magnatab® series for numbers, print, and cursive writing. These toys include a magnetic stylus to write with. As you shape the letters on the plastic writing surface, small steel balls pop up and stick in the outlines of the letters, with audible and tangible pops and clicks. Your child can push the balls back down with her finger when she is finished, again feeling the shape of the letters.

If your Yasmin has high sensory needs, you can try arranging for continuing physical input while Yasmin writes, such as providing a desk-style treadmill so she can walk on it slowly while she is making letters, instead of sitting. A stationary bicycle is another possibility if it leaves her hands free.

Tip # 39: If your Yasmin is ready to learn to write, help her learn simple shapes by giving them meaning right away.

As we have seen earlier in this chapter, *induced communication* is a method for developing a range of communication options. They include helping your child transform scribbles into meaningful graphic symbols. Dr. Miller's description of the strategies for developing graphic symbols for writing appears below.

Remember that writing involves a number of basic shapes your Yasmin needs to know how to make to produce letters. Your task is to make writing come to life at each stage, as she learns each shape. (You may need different shapes for different languages.)

Lines and sticks

Step 1: Yasmin makes meaningless scribbles with a crayon.

Step 2: You help Yasmin make straight lines and circles. (If she is highly motivated, note that she can already write "dog" if she can make three circles in a row, and add a line in the right spot to the first and last circle.)

Step 3: Encourage Yasmin to make a straight line by herself. When she does, immediately put a popsicle stick, a straw, or other straight object beside the line.

Step 4: Make the popsicle stick have some importance. One way is to guide Yasmin to pick up the popsicle stick and poke it into a ball of clay, porcupine style. Do this several times until Yasmin can do it by herself.

Step 5: Show Yasmin a popsicle stick and see if she will represent it with a line. If she does not, help her draw a line, or indicate with a fingertip where she could draw it. When she does, give her a stick for poking into the clay.

Step 6: Try again. This time, when you show Yasmin the popsicle stick, she draws a straight line right away. Hurray! This is representation. Immediately give her the stick.

Circles and discs

Step 7: Yasmin makes a circular shape, either spontaneously or with some guidance.

Step 8: As soon as Yasmin completes a circular shape, you immediately place a disc on that circular shape.

Step 9: The disc needs to come to life! Show Yasmin how to take the disc and place it in a slot in a glass bottle so it drops with a satisfying clink.

Step 10: Soon Yasmin—after completing the circle—will automatically take the disc placed on the circle and drop it in the glass bottle without your support. Try to do this with a series of circle/disc combinations of different sizes and colors.

Step 11: Finally, when you show Yasmin a disc, she will immediately draw the circle. Yes! This is representation. Give her another disc. Try to stop when she is still interested.

If Yasmin is highly motivated, show her she can already write "dog" if she can make three circles in a row, adding a line to the upper right of the first circle and the lower right of the last circle. If she does it, show a real dog, a photo, or a stuffed toy dog right away.

These are the basic shapes needed for lettering. If you want to work with more complicated shapes, consult the instructions in *The Miller Method*® (2007).

More advanced written communication

Many autistic children can benefit from learning the typing keyboard. The advantage of a typewriter over a computer keyboard for sensory-hungry children is that you feel the keys more as you press them.

Typing or keyboarding is a boost to communication for literate kids who find writing difficult, and who may not be able to express their most complex ideas by speaking.

If you have access to the technology or the money, voice input systems on computers to help with writing may make a big difference for your Evan.

Communication for reducing your child's stress

Everyone raising a nonverbal or restricted verbal child with autism at some moment looks into their child's eyes and sees that he is so angry he is about to blow up, but he cannot express this pent-up force.

He may know how to sign "mad," or "angry," but the sign itself may not relieve all the built-up frustrations. He may communicate with pictures or photos, with some precision, and still be angry.

Allow us to pass along a parent's recommendation for tension relief at those times, if your child likes noise.

Explosion therapy

Try building up at least one physical routine that uses your Avery's body in ways he is familiar and successful with, and top it off by making the biggest, loudest, most realistic explosion sound you can produce.

Such as:

Together, you and Avery count to three, signing, with drama, and increasing tension.

Bounce a little on your feet.

Hesitate.

Then yell **BOOOOM**.

Or

Have Avery stamp his left foot, stamp his right foot, slap his left knee, slap his right knee, and clap twice.

You do it with him, forcefully if he tolerates it.

YELL BOOOOOOOM.

Even better if this causes your Avery to yell an approximate "BOOOO" himself.

When you have this routine well practiced, you can ask Avery at any time "Are you angry? Are you mad enough to EXPLODE?! Let's DO it!"

In our house this was so effective it sometimes caused laughter.

Tip # 40: Be aware that some autistic children who have trouble speaking can sing.

Intermezzo

Which is it? A short story about communication

Your Ben has been running water in the big bathtub for several minutes. Happily, he flings his clothes aside and closes the bathroom door behind him.

You hear a little stepping around, you hear a few splashes. Suddenly Ben throws the door open, dashes out of the room scattering water in all directions, and signs in increasing SIZE and EARNESTNESS as he runs away:

"pick up pick up pick up pick up pick up pick up!!!"

Which of the following is true?[9]

  a) He can't find his favorite towel.
  b) He wants you to put away his clothes.
  c) He suddenly remembered he left a popsicle out in the rain.
  d) A chipmunk is swimming in your bathtub, circling the drain.

---

9   If you chose the chipmunk, you are correct. Here is the approved method for getting a chipmunk out of your bathtub without casualties, his or yours: scoop him up in a bucket, leaving just enough water that he cannot get a good foothold to jump out. Walk calmly outside and take him to the nearest woody, rocky spot to pour him carefully out. What if there are no woods near your house, you wonder? Then the cat will not be depositing a chipmunk in your bathtub.

4

HOW TO EXPAND INTERACTIONS, INTRODUCE NEW ONES, AND CAPITALIZE ON DISORDER

The role of order and disorder in expanding our children's abilities

Our children with autism have trouble ordering and making sense of their surroundings and the people with them. Sometimes, this expresses itself in scattered, disconnected behavior; other times, in a tendency for our children to become profoundly involved with one or a few objects or materials, to the exclusion of everything and everyone else.

Used properly, both order and disorder help our children make important intellectual advances that they would not make if only imposed order were the rule. Among the advances our children will make are ever greater interaction with other people and the world.

In Chapter 2, we offered some examples of disorder-created expansions and interruptions to develop coping skills in young children. We also want our children to be able to tolerate expansions in their activities to increase their repertoires for life and to contribute to their cognitive development as they grow up.

For example, a young child ritualistically going down a playground slide over and over, sitting up, may be able to deal with an expansion if you introduce a minor element of variety. Have him throw a small ball down the slide first, and then try sliding down on his stomach or his back. If he is devoted to sliding down sitting up, he may need the reassurance of hand-over-hand assistance to change position, and may appreciate your hand on him as he goes down in the new position.

Expanding interactions can be a long-term challenge for children with ASD, so in this chapter we also offer a few expansions for older or higher-functioning young people.

Suppose your Max is a high-functioning ASD youngster who is fascinated with trains. He is a rapid and intense source of information, but tends toward a monologue, and finds it hard to break out of his favorite subject. Since he is a bright boy and his expertise is enormous, he can literally talk for hours, about trains. You would like Max to be able to switch topics, but he seems unable to let the train topic go.

Tip # 41a: If your high-functioning Max is stuck in a conversation rut, try an expansion of the train topic, or of any other topic your child seems unable to detach himself from.

Examples of expansions:

As Max discusses types of train engines, you speculate with him about where that engine could take the train. This conversation could lead to discussions of rail networks, and distant stations. What would happen if the train reached a national boundary? Perhaps you could shift to technical features of railroad station design, geography and elevation of train stations, signaling systems, switching mechanisms, or typical flora and fauna near the stations.

If you see that you have gone too far afield, you can always return to the discussion of types of train engines for a while, before you try again.

Tip # 41b: Try a substitution of another similar topic, and switch back and forth between them.

Suppose your Max is discussing trains again. You bring up another complex engineering issue, such as how ocean-going ships are built. (Prepare in advance for these talks with your high-functioning Max!) Then, when Max is completely absorbed in ship-building, switch back to train engines. Develop that conversation until a natural opportunity appears to switch back to ships. After you have practiced these conversation changes several times, your Max will now have two types of conversations he enjoys. You can add many more. Eventually Max will have a large repertoire of topics and will no longer be limited to train engines.

Tip # 41c: Consider disagreeing with your high-functioning child if he is speaking *a capella*; switch back to his first position.

If you contradict your Max and he then changes his position to agree with you, you can revert to Max's first position so that he is forced to continue to take into account what you say.

Tip # 42: Stimulate your high-functioning child to develop interactive conversations by showing dramatic responses to what he says.

If your Max, like many high-functioning children with ASD or Asperger's syndrome, does not seem to take his listener, YOU, into account in his discussions, you can help him by showing powerful, vivid reactions to what he says, even venturing to disagree with him at times. Since many children with autism are not aware of the impact they have on others, your notable reactions will help them.

Smile, frown, gesture, shake your head in enthusiasm, in agreement, or disagreement, slap your thigh, applaud, stamp your feet, whistle, etc.

Behavior guidance via expansions and interruptions

You can consider exploring the same strategies for expansions to help guide your child's behavior. In this field manual, we have seen that for coping and for expanding learning opportunities, we use task expansion through mild disorder; task interruption through moderate disorder or low-grade sabotage; and dramatic disorder, a theatrical use of sabotaged routines. With practice, these techniques will help your child cope with change, and enhance his ability to learn. But you can try the same techniques to deal with undesirable behavior.

Example of an interruption to handle upheaval and risky behavior in the car

Suppose your Malika is entranced with car travel, and loves to go for car rides, but sometimes finds the stimulation of passing imagery overwhelming. As she is overwhelmed, with little ability to tell you how she feels, she begins throwing toys or reaching over to pull your hair. Nothing you are able to do while driving seems to calm her.

One approach is to understand that the car ride is a routine, for her, with a beginning and ending point. If you interrupt that routine, her desire to continue it may be strong enough to help her cope. You can say, "Malika, Mom is going to stop." When it is safe to do so, pull over and turn off the engine. If you can do so safely, get out of the car and walk around it once, or walk away a few feet and come back.

Open the door part way and wait for Malika to communicate, to sign "Mom in" or "car go" or something similar. If she does not, you ask her, "Malika wants to go now?" Wait for a nod, a sign, a vocalization, or a word. If you do not get a response right away, prompt it. When you get a response, hop in the car and drive to your destination.

If Malika says no, you can reply, "OK, I will wait a minute and then go."

Capitalizing on disorder: a few words about problem-solving

We want our children on the spectrum to be efficient problem solvers, so that the sensory challenges they already face in life are not complicated by minor snafus. You can bolster their problem-solving abilities by using many physical examples. Here is one for a younger child: With some large blocks or boards cut to a reasonable size, build a long channel on a table top or one side of an Elevated Square. Don't put a roof on it. Make it wide enough for a toy school bus, pickup truck, or other wheeled toy to go through conveniently.

Have your young Oscar stand at one end of the channel, and you at the other. Send the truck back and forth a few times between you to establish what the channel is for. Even better, give Oscar a marble track toy at his end, and send him a few marbles in the pickup truck.

After Oscar becomes interested in that, give him a pile of puzzle pieces for the puzzle you have at your end. When you send Oscar some marbles, zooming the truck through the channel, have him return a puzzle piece for you.

Just as Oscar is getting ready to return the truck to you with a puzzle piece in it, quickly slide one of the blocks or boards out of the wall of your channel and block the truck's passage. "Oh no! A large block in the middle of the channel... BANG! What should we do?"

If Oscar just tries to shove the block out of the way snowplow-style, quickly show him, hand-over-hand if he can tolerate it, how to slide the block back to its previous position, and right away push the truck on through.

Try to do this briskly; taking too much time to remove the barricade can keep Oscar from making the connection between removing the block and having a clear path for his truck.

A more complicated example for a slightly older child: Construction to reach some coveted gummy bears

Before you try this problem-solving session, be sure to teach your child how to make a step or a shelf by putting a plank across two heavy blocks, or stacks of books of equal height. Then show her you can stack these, and can also build ranks of steps. Have a small step stool or stepladder visible in the room.

When you are ready to try problem-solving, while Yael is not looking, pop some of her favorite treats, bright colored gummy bears, into a clear plastic bag and tie them on a string. Suspend the string securely from the ceiling a foot or two higher than Yael can possibly reach.

Have a few large blocks and planks in the room, but only a few near her. Distribute the rest of the blocks and planks around the room, some visible, some perhaps in a closet or behind furniture.

If you don't have a set of large, weight-bearing blocks, use books that can take a bit of abuse, or save up old telephone books, tape two or three together, and collect them til you have a set of six or eight. These are durable and budget-friendly.

Narrate the situation, and ask your child, "Gummy bears are up high. Yael builds?"

If you have a photo of steps constructed with your blocks and planks, try showing her the photo. If it doesn't lead her to start building a step, you help.

Try to arrange it so that Yael is just short of reaching her treats when she has used all the visible blocks and plank(s). Have her step up on the plank, reach up, and see that this is so.

Then tell her more blocks and planks are in the closet, or behind the sofa. Show a photo of the blocks and planks in the closet, if you have one. If necessary, point to the closet. If still no go, partially open the closet door and let Yael do the rest.

Keep on narrating and signing while Yael adds a second step to her structure. Assist if needed, but wait for her attempts. Let her take her time. If she succeeds, fine. If she still needs to build one more step, help her locate those materials as well, by referring to a photo, pointing, or walking near their location.

Celebrate her success when she reaches the goodies. If need be, help her use scissors to cut the bag down.

Next time, if she looks around and locates the stepstool or the ladder and uses it instead to reach her candy, rather than working on construction, good for her! Yael is becoming an efficient problem solver.

Intermezzo

Expansion gone wrong, or You can get that off with Neosporin® first aid cream

Example: Gorilla Tape® athletic supporter.

Your child is calmly working at his computer, comfortably (and fully) attired in sweatpants and a shirt. He is in the middle of a program that takes 45 minutes to complete. So you decamp. You are aware that you have taught him how to use tape, but you do not know he is about to expand that knowledge.

You emerge literally 90 seconds later from the powder room, to a pregnant pause in the kitchen. Weaving a bit on his tiptoes, your son is now standing there naked, except that he is wearing one third of a roll of Gorilla Tape®, structural quality, duct tape, lovingly arrayed about his testicles, coming to a perky point at the tip of his penis. It is well adhered. It looks like a rhinoceros horn. He hands you the bandage scissors, with a hopeful look on his face.

You look around for what is at hand. Peanut butter? Olive oil?

Pondering a trip to the emergency room from which you would full well expect the police to usher you directly to prison, you instead carefully and quickly work antibiotic cream under the tape until it lets go...

5

HOW TO REDUCE CAUSES OF DISTRESS FOR AUTISM SPECTRUM DISORDER KIDS

Causes of distress

Parents, caregivers, and family members notice that their ASD children's anxieties can be caused by many factors. Anxiety often arises from an intense need for predictability. Pain, frustration, fear of failure, and insecurity can contribute to distress, as can unusual sensitivities to sound, light, smell, texture, taste, and sensory hunger for stimulation.

As if that were not enough, your autistic child also deals consciously with much more incoming information than typical children. While a typical child only needs to process 20 percent of all incoming information and sensation consciously, children with autism typically process 80 percent of all information consciously. (Consult your occupational therapist.) They do not develop the normal gating and screening functions that typical children rely on to simplify and interpret the environment.

This matters because it means your Sean probably has delayed processing of sensations and information. You may need to wait calmly for his responses, and if the wait seems overlong, say reassuringly, "When you are ready," or something similar. If you do not recognize Sean's delayed processing, and allow for it, you will distress and frustrate him immensely.[1]

Need for predictability

Your Lucas, because he has acquired autism, may confront many developmental challenges. He may struggle to develop a notion of time, so that reality as Lucas sees it can follow a predictable course. A child lacking this understanding of reality, who lives in a permanent "now," finds it much harder to wait, and to delay the need for his wishes to be gratified instantly.

Tip # 43: If your Lucas has difficulty sequencing, putting things in temporal order, you can give him practice by asking him to arrange photographs in order.

Keep in mind that older children may reject simple sequences such as photos of putting on one sock, then another, then a shoe. More age-appropriate dramatic sequences may be effective for older children. Maybe a child playing baseball! Make it interesting.

This young-man-playing-baseball (or cricket, or soccer) sequence could be set up with three or four interesting pictures without complex backgrounds:

1. pitcher winding up to throw the ball

2. ball in flight toward the batter

3. batter hits ball

4. ball breaks window.

---

1 Processing times can be so extended, especially in younger children, that they can exceed three to five minutes. Try to be patient as you help your child surmount processing delays. One parent reports that her son, with practice and concentration, was able to speed up processing and communication time drastically when he wished to give directions in a moving car.

Then, Lucas's task (with help) is to put the pictures in proper order—perhaps with vivid narration, and sound effects. You can think of many other examples.

Or, having understood sequencing well, your Daniel may depend on unambiguous, unchanging sequences to make his day predictable. Any change in an expected set of events will unnerve him. Help Daniel out by predicting the future for him.

Tip # 44a: Explain changes in routine in a timely way, with illustrations.

Your high-functioning Daniel may be able to accept a change in his school day or a structured day at home if the change is explained at the start of the day in a graphic way, on a whiteboard, on a picture schedule, in a printed social story, or even in a video on his iPad®. To give this explanation the most meaning, first show the usual schedule, and then make the necessary changes.

As you do so, keep an eye on your Daniel to see if he is able to cope with the announcements about changes. You might, for example, erase the "walk in the park" section and replace it with the day's special event, "go to the zoo." Show, with your illustrations and narration, that the rest of the day continues as usual.

Tip # 44b: If this is a temporary change, when the earlier routine is restored, explain the return to it as well, and illustrate it.

For example, you could say, and diagram on the whiteboard, "No zoo trip today, today we are walking in the park."

Sensory hunger as a cause of distress

Remember that unmet sensory needs can be a distress cause all by themselves. Try to maximize your child's sensory input as you see the need. Create opportunities for elevation, including natural ones your child can seize on as needed, such as an elevated fort in a swing set, a safe tree house, climbing equipment at a playground, or a pile of tires in your garden. Encourage your child to jump on a trampoline, roller skate if he is able, ride a scooter or a bike.

Ideally, you should consult an occupational therapist or similar specialist who can assess your Adelle's sensory profile, and suggest what her sensory diet should be. This "diet" is made up of recommended sensory experiences that Adelle needs dependably throughout the day, like food and water. Some children with autism have such keen sensory hunger that they need sensory input often, concurrent with other tasks, perhaps every 15 minutes, and if they are deprived of these sensory stimulations, they suffer.

Unaddressed problems and the origins of aggression

Aggression may be a communication failure in autism, which may not be restrained by the inhibitions a more typical child has absorbed. Your Benjamin may not yet have fully developed empathy; he may not be able to see things from another person's perspective in a way that would allow him to understand the impact of his behavior.

Perhaps your Benjamin is not yet fully able to represent his experience in signs, words, and pictures. Lacking this opportunity to make his views known must at times be very frustrating to him. As he fails to communicate his needs and becomes increasingly agitated, he may lapse into hyper-giggling, flight, or aggressive behavior.

Further, as a result of the biological basis of his autism, he may be for extended periods in a state of adrenaline-pumped fight-or-flight arousal, so for biochemical reasons, he is volatile; it is easy for him to lose his self-control.

Aggression may also occur as a result of an autistic child's colossal need for predictability, as we suggest above. Your Henry may understand and experience the world as a sequence of events that he requires in a predictable order. Consider a well-known adult with autism, the academic Dr. Temple Grandin, who describes her reality as a sequence of video images. If one link in Henry's chain of events is lost, and he does not see how to re-establish connections, he loses his bearings, and may lash out.

So, an adult altering a predictable order of events in Henry's day, without explanation and without an effort to show how order is re-established, will antagonize Henry enormously.

Tip # 45a: Try to view an "attack" as an attempt to make contact.

Try to capture the force of aggression and turn it into meaningful physical contact.

For example, try to intercept a hand attempting to slap you, and turn it into a "high-five" gesture, or, for a smaller child, patty-cake.

Why this works:

If the aggression in the first place was seeking contact, you have provided that contact, and you have at the same time channeled the communicative urge into a socially acceptable way for your child to request contact next time.

Tip # 45b: When possible, turn the aggression into an opportunity to communicate.

You can look puzzled; and ask and sign, "What? Do you need a break?" "Do you need help?"

Tip # 46: Be aware that your autistic child is more vulnerable than a typical child to laughing or giggling inappropriately, not as an expression of humor but to relieve tension.

Why you need a heads-up for this:

Depending on your child, you may need to provide an immediate opportunity for your child to run or jump to deal with the adrenaline. Also, other children and even adults in the vicinity may be unable to accept what they see as your child ridiculing them. Someone is likely to take a swing at your Ben. You may need to observe, "Bennie, when you laugh because you are nervous, sometimes you hurt other people's feelings. Say sorry."

Tip # 47a: If you think your child resorts to hitting when he needs attention or emotional support, try to pre-empt him by maintaining physical contact with him as you turn your attention elsewhere.

Even if you are out in public with limited options, you can still tousle his hair, clap him on the shoulder, give him a quick tickle, or pat him on the head.

If you answer the phone, keep your hand on his, or try to sign to him as you are speaking with someone else. Some parents report the first clear evidence that their ASD child understands signs in just this context, when the child responds to signing that has nothing to do with the ongoing phone conversation.

Tip # 47b: If your Leo tends to slap or hit, make a point throughout the day of engaging him at odd moments in games involving hand clapping and firm physical contact.

If you already ARE engaging him, do it even more.

Routinized hand actions that accompany nursery rhymes or stories, as in "Patty-cake, patty-cake, baker's man... " or "Itsy bitsy spider... " may work well for smaller children. Try to involve your older, stronger child in athletic games which require firm hand contact with a ball, and hand contact with team mates, including claps on the shoulder, congratulations over wins, etc. Contact sports would be good.

Tip # 48: When possible, ignore minor aggression and move on to your next activity.

Why this works:

For small-scale aggression which is intended as communication, such as a minor pinch, ignoring it conveys the message that it was not meaningful, and another line of communication should be opened instead. But this absolutely does not mean to ignore your child. Engage your child immediately as you move briskly to the next activity. Hand him a crayon for coloring, a beanbag to toss, or an apple slice for a snack. You want to change the subject. You do not want to convey the impression that a more enthusiastic pinch would be a better communicator.

When the cause of distress is unknown

Take notes.

If your Tariq can sometimes tolerate a haircut, or a trip to the dentist, and other times suffers a massive meltdown at your destination or on the way, but cannot explain why, try to make a record of every aspect of the successful cases and the unsuccessful ones. When you find reasons that are unique to either the successes or the failures, you are onto something.

Example:

Tariq's father took him to the barber shop for a haircut. Tariq did not accept a cape or a cloth wrapped around his neck. He was wearing a loose polo shirt. He was able to sit still for only a few moments but then began to struggle, and the barber hastily finished a somewhat lopsided haircut. Tariq was fussy on the way home and unable to quiet down completely until after he had had a bath.

The next month, at the same barber, Tariq wore a turtleneck with a close fitting neck. He still refused a cape, but was able to sit calmly through the whole haircut. He was fine for the trip home.

Significant difference: Tariq's shirt. The fact that he was calm after his bath suggests a sensory issue, perhaps unusual smells or sounds that he had to recuperate from, but perhaps also a physical cause which disappeared in the bathwater.

Likely conclusion: hair trimmings down Tariq's shirt made him itch. Use a shirt with a close-fitting neck, or use a piece of adhesive tape to close up the neckline on other shirts, for future haircuts.

Intermezzo
Cinéma vérité: a cause of **YOUR** distress

Your young son is ready for the school bus. He is perfectly clean, his teeth gleam, his hair is glossy, he is wearing a colorful new polo shirt and matching pants, his shoes are shined.

He smiles winningly; you, full of false confidence, duck into the potty for a few urgent seconds.

When you emerge, the bus is here but your son is not. He is in the back yard, naked, covered with dog poo, dancing in the sprinkler.

6

HOW TO STOP A TANTRUM AND RESTORE EQUILIBRIUM: TANTRUM UTILIZATION[1]

Tantrums, severe meltdowns and loss of control happen for varied reasons, sometimes apparently exploding out of nowhere. Try to remain calm and relaxed. Try not to be intimidated. Your elevated emotional state will spread to your child, and cue her that she *should* be concerned.

Try to understand the meaning of the tantrum or loss of control, since this varies from child to child, from event to event, and may require creative solutions. One child may have a tantrum because she cannot cope with the shift from one situation to another, and she needs help to do so. Another child's loss of control may be triggered by sensory starvation when he stays seated too long, or, alternatively, from sensory overload from discordant sounds, flickering lights, or intense smells. Still another child's tantrum or collapse into passivity may stem from a feeling of abandonment triggered by a parent or carer turning their attention to another child, or by the loss of a treasured object.

Transitions (including coping with dramatic change), sensory starvation, sensory overload, and loss can all cause

---

1   This commentary in a different form (Miller with Chrétien 2007) was previously published by Jessica Kingsley and appears here with the gracious permission of the publishing house.

tantrums or withdrawal. Pain, frustration, and failure to communicate may also be causes.

In the chaos of severe tantrums—screaming, thrashing around, arms flailing, legs kicking, perhaps objects breaking— our children may be out of contact with their bodies and with everyone trying to help them. At other times, they may fall into extreme passivity, described vividly by Dr. Miller (Miller with Chrétien 2007, p.215) as the "beached whale syndrome."

We view both catastrophic tantrums and deep withdrawal as a failure in the child's ability to cope with people, objects, or the sensory impact of the environment. We can understand these situations in two forms, those that are largely involuntary, or those that are largely social and communicative, with many strategies for gaining control over them and for calming our children.

In keeping with Miller's strategy of using the forces of ASD compulsions and obsessions, we will also try to use the features of the tantrum to shape it and bring it under control.

Tip # 49a: First, try to understand the cause from your child's point of view, ruling out pain and injury as quickly as possible.

Example:

One parent recounts that her young son dashed in from the back yard screaming, flailing, kicking, and howling. He could not point to any injuries. A superficial check revealed no problems, other than the usual grime, and in rapid succession the boy refused food, candy, gum, and a drink, his normal centering items, as he spun increasingly out of control. Since this child often could calm down in the bath, the mother put him in the bathtub and examined him more closely. When his hair was wet, three hornet stings could be seen glowing on the top of his head.

Tip # 49b: Understand complex causes.

Example:

Another parent described a child's tantrum in a department store, evidently caused by losing balloons. The seven-year-old child on the autism spectrum had let go of his two helium balloons, which promptly and irretrievably sailed 20 feet to the ceiling. The parent swiftly replaced them with two more of the same color, but the substitution did not succeed. The child kept yelling, "Need help!" his favorite stock phrase, and lost control, yelling and hitting as the parent tried to extricate him from the store. This parent reported, "I had done everything I could think of. I stretched my arms up and said, 'It's too high; I can't get it,' and I had given him two more. Why didn't this work?"

Dr. Miller's view:

Getting the two balloons of the same color and giving them to your son was absolutely correct! But for your son, the problem might not have been loss of the balloons themselves, but his inability to recapture them. Recreating his original experience of balloons floating away, except that this time the balloons were tethered to a much longer string, so that your son could pull on the string to reel them back, might have made the difference.[2] While hauling the new balloons in, the boy could overcome the feeling of loss of the first two balloons, because the second pair of balloons with the longer

---

2   The compiler notes that this suggestion implies if you are going to buy balloons, you should carry a ball of string around in your pocket. Other possibilities include tying a small weight to the balloon string in the first place, tying it to the child's wrist, or tying it to a shopping cart.

strings attached could provide a corrective experience, which would complete his expectations and would emphasize his power to act in the world.

The child's disappointment and inability to accept that a request for help could not result in the help he wanted might be factors here as well.

Tantrum utilization

Over the years the Millers, Dr. Callahan, and the staff of the LCDC developed a number of strategies which help children reorganize themselves and resolve their tantrums. These strategies—known as tantrum utilization—help the child by drawing on the different parts of his/her tantrums. Here are the main elements of tantrum utilization:

Tip # 50: Narrate your child's tantrum.

One utilization strategy—effective with children who understand a fair amount of spoken language—is narrating the child's tantrum. Here, the parent or caregiver might say, "Daniel is very upset. He is kicking his feet, crying, screaming, and banging his fists on the ground... Now he is kicking, now screaming... Will he bang his fists now and then scream? No, he is kicking and then screaming. What will he do next? Oh, yes, he is banging his fists."

Often with this kind of narration, a child will pause in the tantrum to listen to what the parent is saying. The child, too, becoming aware of his/her own behavior, becomes curious about what his or her body is doing, and more able to exert control.

As this occurs, the intensity of the tantrum subsides, and soon the parent is able to say, "Daniel feels better now. A big hug and go play."

Why this works:

It helps the child bring himself into complete voluntary control because it names the parts of the tantrum and breaks it up, giving the child the vocabulary to understand the event. It provides attention to him without endorsement or criticism, increases the child's awareness of receptive language and of its meaning in the world, and enhances relationships.

Tip # 51a: Divide and conquer.

In this two-part tactic, try discouraging one part of the tantrum, while continuing to request another: "No screaming." "Kick! Kick more!"

You can also give a series of rapid, gross motor commands such as, "Sit down!" or, "Stand up!" Then, when your child is able to comply, divide the tantrum into parts and ask for one part at a time, such as, "Just kick! Kick more!"

In this kind of tantrum utilization, the carer, parent, or other family member takes an active role in directing the tantrum.

Example:

Nathan, faced with a request to work, begins jumping, kicking, and screaming. In the midst of his tantrum, his mother, pointing to the floor, firmly says, "Sit down!" When Nathan sits down, she demands, "Get up!" She repeats this sequence several times.

Some children will regain control at this point.

If Nathan sits down still screaming and kicking, his mother then tries a division of the tantrum again, saying, "No screaming...just kicking!" and next, with hand motions or signs simulating kicking, says, "Kick, kick, kick!" As the boy responds to his mother's request that he kick, the quality of his kicking begins to change. Kicking that Nathan might not previously have been fully conscious of now comes under the constraint of the parent's language. At this point, his mother may direct Nathan to get up and walk around a defined or elevated space, or try some other quieting activity. Nathan is already much calmer and more directed.

Tip # 51b: Variation: divide, conquer, and count.

For children who know that many events regularly take place on the count of three, you may be able to help a child bring herself under conscious control in a tantrum by counting in your instructions.

Example:

"Sophie, scream! Scream more! One, two, three: now kick."

Why this can work:

While listening to the counting, Sophie has already quietened a bit; making the effort to be able to wait and listen, and then kick on command. Predictably, when she thinks things should happen (on the count of three), she is already regaining self-control.

Tip # 51c: Divide, conquer, and communicate.

Use the screaming component of a tantrum to stop the tantrum while helping a nonverbal child learn to control his voice.

When Harry is having a tantrum, his father says, "Sit down!" and, "Get up!" Just as Harry starts to scream, the father tells Harry to scream, touching Harry's mouth to indicate where the scream comes from. Often your child will emit a small sound, or even a full-bodied yell, which you can encourage.[3] Again, by having Harry reproduce screaming at his father's request, screaming which Harry previously emitted without full control or awareness is now responsive to the father's direction. It becomes controllable, and the developing control of vocal cords contributes to the nonverbal child's conscious production of sounds.

Some children with ASD may be able to gain vocal control rapidly, and deliberately become quiet when asked to scream. This may be a way of saying "no" to the parent, and in any case helps the tantrum dissipate. Note that we welcome and try to encourage the communication that a tacit "no" implies. The parent can ask, if his child is attentive, "Does Harry say no?"

Tantrum abatement under these conditions is often very rapid.

Tip # 52: Try reciprocal screaming in a mild or moderate tantrum.

Although this may seem crazy, reciprocal screaming can actually help stop a mild tantrum. Suppose your Andrew finds a shift to a new routine objectionable and protests with loud screams, but he is otherwise not too out of control. At this point, Andrew's mother may say, "First Andrew screams, then Momma screams," and then she repeats her child's scream. Some children will laugh at this point, and the tantrum evaporates.

If you need to continue, after an exchange or two, you could add to this reciprocal screaming the tactic of pointing to the person who is screaming, to emphasize the turn-taking aspect.

---

3   If your child is nonverbal, encourage ALL vocalizations, no matter how apparently improper or inconvenient.

Reciprocal screaming may be repeated several times until you pounce on an opportunity to vary the activity, "Andrew screams and then pushes the car down the ramp," or, "Andrew screams and then throws the ball," or another suitable expansion. Typically, after a few turns at reciprocal screaming, your child will comply with your request in an organized manner and will no longer find it necessary to scream.

This particular method of tantrum utilization is most effective with relatively minor tantrums. Its effectiveness, Dr. Miller speculated, comes from the child feeling heard, understood, and taken seriously by the parent or other adult who repeats the child's scream. Be careful that you do not accidentally sound satirical; your Andrew may well be sensitive to intonation and intention. Such interaction may also serve as a welcome transition for the child, who may then feel ready to follow your directions in other ways.

Tip # 53: Try plucking at your child's clothing while pulling him gently off-balance.

This is most effective for younger children.

This tactic may be especially effective when your child is small and you think a sensory deficit may be the main problem. The object here is not to make him fall down, but to move his center of gravity enough that he has to engage his body awareness to regain his balance.

Why this works:

Some tantrums are genuinely losses of control, caused by failure of predictability or by falling off the sensory roller coaster that is autism. They are not deliberate tactics to communicate. The child urgently wishes to regain self-control but cannot. Tugging on clothing gives some surface skin sensation, and helps the child regain volitional control of his body as he reorients to avoid falling. Because you have provided a smaller increment to regaining control, just reorienting to his center of gravity, he is able then to control the larger sensory issues and stop throwing a tantrum.

Variations for a smaller child include dropping and catching her, in your lap, or, for a larger child, leaning him strongly to one side.

Tip # 54: Sleuth around: do the detective work to find the root of a tantrum.

Loss of contact, or loss of prized objects, are frequent causes of persistent problems. Sometimes a child on the spectrum, who has been progressing nicely over a period of months, begins to tantrum at every change in the day's school program or any change in the usual activities at home. He has HAD enough. But why? When such a sudden shift in the child's conduct occurs, try several of the practical tips mentioned above, and then explore any possible changes that may have taken place at home or school, which may not have made much of an impression on the adults.

Concerned about one such child, Oliver, and his sudden loss of ability to cope, Dr. Miller interviewed Oliver's mother. Dr. Miller noted that Oliver had been unusually irritable in school. Every change in the program seemed to set him off. Dr. Miller wondered whether there had been any recent changes at Oliver's house. Were relatives visiting? Had new children arrived? Was there a new baby, a new dog, or had old neighbors moved away? Oliver's mother assured Dr. Miller that nothing had changed in those respects. Dr. Miller than asked whether either of the parents' schedules had changed. This turned out to be a revealing question.

Oliver's mother acknowledged that in fact her family had seen a distinct schedule change; her husband had switched to the night shift. When he had worked the day shift, he regularly rough-housed with his son Oliver, but now that he worked nights, he had to rest during the day and was not available at their usual hours for the rough-housing sessions so important to his son.

Dr. Miller suggested that the parents try to work out a way for Oliver to enjoy that rough-housing contact with his father during a different part of the day. Restoring rough-housing might make all the difference in whether Oliver was able to stay composed at school

Subsequently, Oliver's father resumed rough-housing with him, and school tantrums diminished dramatically.

Why regular rough-housing with parents and other friends and relatives works: it emphasizes emotional bonds, in this case between father and son; it meets the boy's sensory need for deep pressure; it restores order and routine in his world so he can feel comfortable.

Try not to cause a tantrum unnecessarily. Some children with autism prize particular objects, and if the precious object must be removed for some reason, perhaps to be washed, an enormous tantrum can be forecast. If you MUST remove your child's precious baby lamby to wash it, because the stench it is emitting exceeds the standards you can tolerate, try to trade it quickly for something similarly prized. If there is nothing similarly prized, try to remove it while your beloved child is sleeping.

Beaching, and what to do about it

Certain children with autism, generally larger and heavier ones, flop down on the floor, refuse to move, and passively resist all efforts to be moved or to be engaged in communication or work. These children, like beached whales, have lost their ability to navigate. They are stranded. While not a tantrum, this "beached whale syndrome" can present difficulties for parents and caregivers alike, since it similarly hinders ordinary life and work with the child and might be unsafe in public places.

Adults are tempted to respond with irritation and frustration when a child in their care ignores their commands, but the child is simply too large to compel. You cannot simply pick him up and get on with it.

Having worked with several such stranded children, Dr. Miller found that part of their motivation for beaching was often a wish for more nurturing and more attention. Accordingly, he recommended that adults dealing with "a beached whale" should not attempt to lift the child,[4] but instead should stay calm and carry on with the work at hand.

Tip # 55a: For beaching, crouch down next to the beached child and talk to him quietly, while gently rubbing his back or patting him for about five minutes. Talk simply and directly about some topic of mutual interest.

Next, stand up slowly and, without saying a word, simply hold out a hand.

In almost every instance, a "beached whale" treated this way will accept a proffered hand and allow himself to be led back to the family.

---

4   Dr. Miller had only seen beaching with boys, but Dr. Smith has seen several cases with girls. And we are reliably informed by Jennifer Cavalli, Director of Student Services at Crotched Mountain School in Greenfield, New Hampshire, that beaching is an equal opportunity tactic.

Tip # 55b: For beaching, try humor and physical affection.

Parents report that humor combined with affection may also work. In one case, older parents, observing their apparently hibernating son, crouched down beside him, prodding him gently and tickling him, while exclaiming, "What? Passive resistance? Son, we are the generation of 1968! We practically INVENTED the passive resistance! Ha Ha! So THERE!" This attention and banter eventually got a giggle out of the young man, who hopped to his feet and went out to play.

Tip # 56: If the child is not too large, and two muscular adults are present, treat beaching by swinging.

While talking calmly to the child, have one adult pick up the child's hands and another his feet, to swing him gently back and forth a few inches above the ground. You could also try singing a simple song to the rhythm of swinging.

Variation: Float your stranded whale.

If he is not too large, so Dr. Miller's concern about lifting might not apply, take a tip from those rescuing stranded sea mammals and slip a blanket under your beached whale to "float" him.[5] Float and swing him gently on the blanket for a few minutes, or as long as your strength holds out.

Why this works:

These tactics of engagement meet the child's need for affection and emotional as well as physical support.

---

5   To get the blanket under him, you can roll him carefully sideways as per making a hospital bed with the patient still in it.

Sometimes, parents and other stressed care givers suffer from a tendency to dismiss beaching and the child's need for nurturing by saying, "Oh, he just does that for attention!"

Of course he does! He needs attention just as we need oxygen.

Consider how wonderfully well you have succeeded if your child has progressed from a detached state, in which he could not express interest in you, to one in which he can show you how much he needs you. Give him a kiss.

How to re-establish equilibrium and work to prevent future problems

Sometimes, as you see your child with autism becoming edgy and beginning to lose her composure, you can intervene to help her de-escalate, to prevent a tantrum from precipitating. Other times, after a tantrum has subsided, your child may not have been able to relax and regain total control. In both cases, you can often lead your children to re-establish complete equilibrium by increasing communication with you, by increasing or adjusting their sensory input, and by routinizing their responses to unexpected disconcerting events. Try some of these options.

Tip # 57: Try mimicking the sounds your child makes, then end it all...

If your child is beginning to lose her composure and is yelling, try mimicking her sounds for several seconds or more in a sympathetic way, perhaps with a gradual decrescendo, and then give a firm command accompanied by a sign, such as "stop," "enough," or "all done."

Why this can work:

It conveys to your Dahlia that you hear, appreciate, and understand her problem, you sympathize, but also, enough is enough.

Tip # 58: If your Ben is beginning to spin out of control, try helping him regain self-control by ordering him to lie down or sit down and then get up again rapidly on request.

As per tantrum utilization, you may need several repetitions for this to work, but even the first time may help your child relax.

Tip # 59: Try to vary the environment when your child begins to lose control. For example, change the sound of your voice.

Shift your voice quality, tone, or volume; shout, or whisper, depending on what contrasts the most with what you were doing before.

Sometimes it is enough to offer your child a drink, preferably with a distraction such as an unusual cup, a straw, or bubbles. Drinking is very centering. Hard chewing gum helps children with intense sensory needs because it gives deep pressure at the jaw joint.

Re-establish your child's composure with several varieties of sensory input

Tip # 60a: Restore your child's fragile equilibrium by giving more sensory input, such as firm hugging, or holding his hands and flapping his arms loosely sideways.

Other examples of calming and refreshing techniques:

For a small child, holding the child firmly in an embrace while talking in a quiet tone may be effective. You can also try reciprocal face touching, and hair stroking. Use your Alicia's hand to touch her face, then yours, identifying her and you. Say her name, and yours, as you do so. (See the more complete discussion below.)

Your Isabella will get a lot of sensory input if you take her hands, and use them to flap her arms sideways several times.

Variations:

If your child calms down in the bath but begins to lose control afterwards, you can try after the bath putting a terrycloth bathrobe on her and tying the sash firmly.

Some children will request multiple robes with multiple tightly tied sashes. These children are craving pressure. Pressure-craving children may also benefit from weighted clothing, or wrist and ankle weights which can be easily removed or varied often. Elastic clothing such as bicycle shorts or clothing that wraps and ties with some small amount of pressure may help. Narrow spaces to crawl through, fabric tunnels, small sleeping bags, and squeeze machines could all be helpful.

You can consider swaddling or using a cradle board for very young children who need to feel pressure. If they are still quite small, consider carrying them with you in slings across your chest or in baby backpacks.

You can also try, especially for younger children, destabilizing them just as you did for tantrum abatement, by plucking at their clothes just enough to require them to regain balance. This often leads to regained self-control.

Tip # 60b: Try a complete whole body application of deep pressure.

For sensory-craving children, have an occupational therapist teach you how to give the child deep joint pressure, starting with the child seated in your lap or on the floor between your knees. The occupational therapist can show you how to work down from the head and neck through all the major joints, even to flexing fingers and toes.

Tip # 60c: Ask the sensory-craving child to carry heavy objects, move furniture, or wear a backpack loaded with heavy books.

Tip # 60d: Don't forget the power of rough-housing.

Tip # 60e: For sensitive children with autism, try light massage, lotion, or skin brushing.

Some children do not benefit from heavy input and deep pressure because of their sensitivities. If your Aubrey has well-developed skin sensitivities, she may prefer a light massage, use of lotions or powders, skin brushing with a soft bristly surgical brush, or even stroking her skin with a delicate make-up brush.

Tip # 60f: Mutual face touching, with several repetitions, can re-establish a child's self-control.

What to do:

Take your Michael's hands, and use them alternately to stroke first his face and then your face. If you can add sounds without upsetting Michael, when you are using his hand to stroke his face, say his name. Then, when you take his hand and encourage him to stroke your face, identify yourself, saying "Dad," Mom," "Nana," or "Emma," etc., as the case may be. Start out slowly, then speed up, and abruptly blow on Michael's hand, or, if you feel like it, pretend to nibble on his fingers.

Why increasing or adjusting sensory input works:

Tactics like hugging satisfy the children's sensory hunger, and can release neurotransmitters. They also reassure the child that nothing disastrous is happening, increase your emotional bond, and thus diminish insecurity.

Re-establish equilibrium with tactics to restore order and express the desire for completion

You will often be able to make unexpected events acceptable to your child with autism by incorporating into your child's repertoire a routine response to change. Over time, with practice, these routines can accumulate and help make him more flexible.

Tip # 61a: Involve your Chloe in a simple, repetitive routine to restore her composure.

Use simple, repetitive routines to restore composure, such as sorting silverware into a tray, or sorting socks into a drawer.

You want a well-defined beginning and end, so that the child feels completion.

What to do:

For one example, lead your Chloe by the hand to the silverware drawer, and show her the basket of clean silverware to be sorted. If she does not begin on her own, hand a spoon or a fork to her and point to the correct spot. When she is focused, continue handing her spoons and forks as fast as she sorts them. She may wish to do it all herself then. Adjust your pacing to your own child's needs.

Why repetitive routines work:

Repetitive routines allow Chloe to fulfill her intense desire for order, predictability and completion. Further, they reinforce her sense of herself and her power to cause events in the world.

A more complex example:[6]

An autistic child may be afraid of events over which you have little to no control, such as shifts in the weather, storms, and temporary loss of electricity or running water. If your Aiden is unnerved by a power failure, but is able to maintain enough composure to pay attention, try this:

Tip # 61b: Narrate the current conditions, and offer options of order-restoring routines.

To help your child cope with dramatic events over which you have no control, offer order-restoring routines he favors. If your child is verbal, use simple and direct language. Sign too as you narrate, if possible, if your child is nonverbal.

---

6   This example appears courtesy of speech therapist extraordinaire Lynn Medley, M.S., CCC-SLP, of Ft Washington, PA, in the US.

One set of "current crisis conditions" for Aiden:

1. Sometimes the lights go out. No power. No TV.

2. Mom and Dad say, "Oh no!" and Aiden is scared.

3. Mom and Dad understand. They call the power company. The repair truck will come.

While Aiden is waiting, he can resort to several physical outlets for his concern, and to some routines to help him regain calm:

I. Opportunities to use his body to dispel anxiety:

• Stamp several times, perhaps while you count, sing a song, or recite a nursery rhyme Aiden knows (these add structure and predictability for him).

• Close doors.

• Push in chairs to the table, or arrange furniture.

• Carry the trash out.

• Play tiddlywinks or jumping frogs.

II. Opportunities to replace the lost sensation and increase engagement, change the subject away from the power outage, and increase ability to cope:

• Listen to the battery-powered radio or CD player.

• Turn on flashlights.

• Watch a movie or listen to music on his (charged) laptop computer.

• Play a video game.

• Play a harmonica.

III. Something to do when calm is restored:

- Take a nap.

- Have a snack.

- Take a bath.

Tip # 62a: Try to use the force of the child's reaction to the order-shattering event to increase communication.

For example, you can try to prompt your limited verbal child to actually say an, "Oh, no!" along with the parents' exclamation of dismay, "Thunder? Lights out!"

Tip # 62b: For longer-term stability, rank order your Aiden's crisis events from most to least severe. You will use this ranking as a basis for communication.

For the longer term, try to rank the events that your child perceives as a crisis, so that he can use this ranking to compare future events and communicate with you about their severity. When time permits, make a cardboard illustration with photos, drawings, words, and/or numbers to represent the degree of severity of the event to your child.

In Aiden's case, a wheel falling off a toy car was a crisis which had to be remedied promptly, but it was not too severe. It might be a one on Aiden's crisis scale. It might be represented by a green light. A toy helicopter whose batteries had died, so that the blade would not rotate and the lights would not flash, Aiden experienced as a more severe event requiring an immediate fix, perhaps a three on the crisis scale, and a yellow light. The most terrible event on Aiden's crisis scale was a loss of electric power, which he felt should have had an instantaneous fix, perhaps represented by a five and a red light.

In future, when Aiden is upset, his parents can point to the scale and ask: "How bad is it? Is it as bad as the dead helicopter?" etc. Some children may respond to images of faces to convey degrees of concern on their crisis charts.

This imagery helps your Aiden move toward fuller communication and more abstract use of ideas.

Summary

In this chapter, we are not talking about deliberate tantrums sometimes used by typical children as a bargaining device. Although some ASD kids' tantrums have a clear communicative element, here we are discussing loss of control among ASD children due to the nature of their autism.

In every case, we want to use the forces of the tantrum to shape it and to teach the children to control themselves, by capturing the tantrum activity, directing it and routinizing it, thus spending its force and directing its remaining energy into other channels.

We do not simply forbid tantrums and beaching, because prohibitions do not work.

Intermezzo

Generalizations about round white porcelain: dryer cycle number one

Your kid is playing outside so you quickly start supper. As you serve it, you notice an unnatural silence upstairs. The kid has slipped quietly in and out again.

The washer has been reset. (Extra rinse, OK.) The dryer door is open. The light glows warmly on a golden pool in the bottom of the dryer drum.

Your kid has peed in the dryer.

7

HOW TO FOSTER FRIENDSHIPS

Your severely affected child on the autism spectrum may not be able to make friends by himself as readily as his typical siblings or classmates. And do not be surprised if he has just as much trouble forming bonds with other people with autism as anyone else might. Children with autism whose sensory needs are in opposition are particularly unlikely to be able to form friendships with each other. If every time your sensory-craving Kai slams some cymbals together happily, his classmate Cara runs away crying and holding her ears, those two are not a match made in heaven.

You may find that your Eitan relates much more easily to typical people, or to Downs syndrome people, than to other children with autism. He may find it easier to relate to one gender, or to people of varied ethnicities from his.

Eitan may need to be taught some play skills, and how to relate to other children. You can help show him how to take turns, how to reciprocate, how to join and leave a group, and how to participate in controlled competition.

You can help him create connections with many sorts of people. If your Graham is an example of a guy who needs to be taught how to relate to other kids, you might try some of these tips.

Tip # 63: Model meeting and greeting gestures.

Teach your Jacob to give high fives, to wave hi and bye, namaste, or whatever gestures are appropriate and current in your community.

Tip # 64: For your nonverbal child seeking friends, teach common gestures for communication such as thumbs up, OK, V for victory, applause, and blowing kisses.

Concentrate on gestures actually used by young people in your area. You may need an informant if you don't have nephews and nieces of appropriate ages.

Tip # 65: Children with autism can build bonds with one another with deep pressure, if they crave it.

Naturally this will not work if your Rukhmini is hypersensitive rather than hyposensitive and does not like squeezes. But if your Ben loves to start every day with a big hearty hug from Roberto, who squeezes him and lifts him off the floor, those boys are laying the groundwork for a beautiful friendship.

Tip # 66: If your Remy does not already know how to take turns, help her learn by having her alternate anything she likes to do with another child.

If she enjoys building with blocks, have her take turns with a classmate or neighbor building together—first Remy puts a block on, then Alice adds one. If you have a swing set with only one swing, Remy and Drew can take turns swinging and pushing. Narrate "Remy's turn! Now it's Drew's turn!"

This is also a productive time to elicit speech from a child struggling to talk.

Some swing sets come with a two-person glider the children can sit on face-to-face. This is effective for learning about interactions with other people, since one child's pushing on the footrest moves the other child's footrest back, encouraging awareness of what the other child is doing, and encouraging participation and turn-taking to make the glider start to swing.

Playground equipment requiring two people, such as see-saw, can also help build relationships and trust.

Some parents report success teaching turn-taking and interaction by using a toy called a Zoom Ball. This toy consists of a hollow plastic ball shaped a bit like a USA football, through which two nylon cords run. One child holds the cords at one end, one in the left hand and one in the right, while another child holds the cords at the other end. As your Ben pulls his cords apart, the friction on the ball propels it toward Ben's neighbor Bobby. Zip! When the ball arrives, Bobby returns it to Ben by pulling his cords briskly out to the side. In one version, the ball can carry a water balloon that will pop when the ball stops abruptly. The sibilant sound as the ball travels along the cords may be alluring to some children.

You can build relationships by creating many structured opportunities for interaction. Here are some possibilities:

Tip # 67a: Teach your ASD child to interact with other children by helping them take turns bringing each other snacks, or drinks on a tray.

You might start simply with only two or three children and three pretzels, gradually working up to ice cream bars or glasses of lemonade.

Tip # 67b: Help your Carter build friendships with his playgroup by showing them how to stick bits of masking tape or colored stickers on each other's faces, with your suggestions.

Examples:

"Now the nose! Carter, try a cheek? Ruby, put tape on Ben's ear!" Masking tape bits are likely to elicit giggling and laughter. Teach the "ha ha" sign if the opportunity arises. Have them take turns taking each other's tape bits off.

On a hot day, if you are outside, substitute water toys that squirt, or ice cubes.

Tip # 67c: Try to get ball games going using a suspended ball.

Your young Alex may be able to play ball more easily with another child using a tetherball or a ball suspended from the ceiling, that follows a predictable arc.

Then expand and diversify the sorts of games your child can play.

Tip # 68: Try tug-of-war games with a soft rope with knots on it.

Children with autism who like deep pressure may spontaneously create and enjoy informal tug-of-war games, and the game can include any number of children the rope will allow. Try making a startlingly colored line on the ground for the children not to cross as they pull.

Tip # 69: Play the "I'm going to GET you!" game to lay the basis for tag games.

You can teach your child the basics of tag games for later if you start while he is young and interested in being tickled.

Threaten to catch him and tickle him if he doesn't run away, by towering over him making a monster face, and pronouncing, "I am going to get you!"

When your Oliver runs away chortling and looks over his shoulder to see how close you are to catching him, your game is going well! Just before you catch him, suddenly bolt away in the opposite direction. If Oliver tries to catch you, your game has become reciprocal and will transfer readily to playing tag games with other children. Guess who is "IT" now!

Tip # 70: Teach your child to play hide and seek.
When your Jonquil is absorbed in a game with her grandmother, quietly slip away and hide without Jonquil noticing. When you are hidden, Grandma, in on your tricks, asks Jonquil, "Where is Daddy? Go find Daddy!" and then Grandmother begins to look for you everywhere where you are not. Is Dad in the closet? He is not. Is Dad in the cupboard? Certainly not! You want your Jonquil to get up and actively look, with Grandmother. When Daddy is found, have Momma hide, or Auntie JB, or anyone else in on the plan. Celebrate each time you find someone, with loud approval and applause. Finally, Momma and Jonquil hide together, and Daddy has to look everywhere for them.

Ultimately, Jonquil will be able to hide by herself, but she will need practice. First she will need to hide with someone else, to get the idea.

Tip # 71: Teach your Taufiq to notice and comment on his friends' appearance or skills.
Example:
"See Leon's blue shirt? Beautiful!" or, " Look at Isaac's slam-dunk! Wow! He is FAST!"

Tip # 72: Ask your child's teacher to pair your Eitan with a regular buddy at school.

For group activities at school, even if it is only moving furniture, carrying books, or emptying the trash, your Eitan can build relationships by doing things together predictably with the same person.

Intermezzo

Law of inverse affect

Your child has begun to dispose of his shoes outdoors by throwing them into the woods.

Late one autumn afternoon, as the sun casts its last yellow light low through the branches, he tosses his only pair of shoes over the fence.

You find one immediately, but the other has vanished in the depths of the foliage.

Where, in a hundred feet of deciduous forest, could it be? You search, as the light fades, with a flashlight. The bats come out, the moon rises. Hopeless. How can your son go to school the next day?

Chagrined, you slink into the house. But suddenly, you remember! You are saved by the law of inverse affect!

As you will recall, the law of inverse affect states that the probability of an event is inversely proportional to its affect. Events you dread have a high probability. Events you pine for have a low probability.

So where is the shoe? In the most inconvenient spot possible! Since you do not have an open well, that would be the hollow tree cut off six feet above the ground. Therefore, the shoe must be inside the hollow tree cut off six feet above the ground. Rest easy!

Early the next morning, you stroll into the back yard toward the woods. You don't even bother to notice that there is no shoe on the ground and no shoe in the shrubbery: you climb up on some logs and peer down into the hollow tree.

And there is the shoe.

8

HOW TO INCREASE FAMILY CONNECTIONS: WHAT YOU CAN DO AT HOME

A physical and emotional sense of self for your ASD child

Begin considering how to deepen warm family ties by building a sturdy sense of self for your autistic child, with Miller Method® strategies.

The problem:

Children with autism do not experience their bodies in the same way typical children do, because in many cases they have lost some transmission of sensory impulses from the body to the brain, and pathways carrying instruction from the brain back to the body may also be affected.

And that isn't all. Many children with autism have not been able to integrate vision, hearing, smell, their sense of touch, taste, and other sensory experiences into one coherent whole of sensory experience. Because of the enormous undifferentiated sensory barrage that they live with, they may have difficulty paying attention to more than one sense at a time, and therefore may choose to focus on only one, as Tito Mukhopadhyay, mentioned below, chose to favor hearing. Other children may favor vision, becoming hypervigilant visually, naturally detecting tiny variations around them, such as loose bolts in playground equipment or a nearly invisible scar on a new therapist's hand, where his sixth finger was amputated at birth. Children with sensory integration problems or hypervigilance may lose their tempers easily. They may deal with crossover of sensory experience that humans do not normally experience,[1] such as hearing in color, tasting sounds, etc.[2]

If your Nieves seems to struggle with these phenomena, she needs sensory integration occupational therapy.

Children who acquire autism may lose speech, or the ability to go up and down stairs, or may be hindered in many other ways from full use of their bodies. They may fight to acquire full reception of feeling from all parts of their bodies, and they may flounder while attempting to categorize, understand, and use input from all of their senses.

One result, besides the obvious fear and frustration, is that they may have difficulty locating pain in their bodies and—in extreme cases—may even lose the sense that they inhabit physical bodies. Tito Rajarshi Mukhopadhyay, a severely autistic young man, has written about his early experience trying to increase his own sense of self:

> When I was four or five years old, I hardly realized that I had a body except when I was hungry or when I realized that I was standing under the shower and my body got wet. I needed constant movement, which made me get the feeling of my body. The movement can be of a rotating

---

1   If you suspect your child suffers from these conditions, consult an occupational therapist.
2   Probably these conditions have a biological basis but not all are known. It is known, for example, that failure of rod function in the eye can cause many of the visual aberrations in autism, but that problem can be alleviated with the vitamin A that occurs in fish liver oil.

type or just flapping of my hands. Every movement is a proof that I exist.[3]

To build strong self-concepts for our children, we must first help our children on the autism spectrum feel the substantial nature of their bodies. As Dr. Miller has noted in his work with Kristina Chretien (Miller and Chrétien 2007), the growing sense of self builds on body awareness.

In addition, we need to do everything in our power to help our children come to terms with living on a sensory roller coaster, and to develop a concept of themselves as social beings in relationships with others. Evaluation for occupational therapy is critical, particularly to identify your child's own individual sensory profile, hyper- and hyposensitivities.

Tip # 73a: If you have a hyposensitive child with autism, build his body awareness by bombarding him with sensation.

Many strategies help children like Tito build adequate body awareness. Among them are "rough and tumble" play, tickling, restabilizing, and face-touching. Used effectively, they also include "teasing" ("I'm going to get your nose, etc." or, with another person, having a playful tug of war over the child's body: "I want that foot…I want that arm!"). Chasing games and contact sports are highly recommended, as well as unexpected interruptions, to build body anticipation of what is going to happen next.

You can also help enhance your hyposensitive autistic child's body awareness by encouraging him to push, pull, lift, and carry heavy objects from one place to another. Depending on his size and strength, he can help rearrange

---

3   See *The Mind Tree* (2011) and *How Can I Talk if My Lips Don't Move* (2011), both published by Arcade Publishing.

furniture, stack books, carry bags of farm animal feed, grass seed, or mulch; roll out a large trash can, carry groceries, and be helpful in many ways that also contribute to your household.

Each time your Thomas uses his body to cope with the resistance of objects, he experiences his body as an effective tool, and experiences himself as an effective agent. So, Thomas has demonstrated to himself the capacity of his body to do things (body efficacy), and has begun to establish the substantial nature of his body.

If your Derek needs more sensation, you can add to his sensations by choosing clothing, bedding, and towels that provide feedback. You can encourage him to sleep with a sheepskin against his skin. You can provide him flannel sheets and nubby towels. You can use heavily textured clothing, and you can add a weighted vest, or wrist or ankle weights, from time to time. (These weights need to be removed about every half an hour or the body adjusts to them and they lose effect. Needless to say, never use weighted blankets or other weights to control or punish your child.)

Be aware that even though your David needs intense sensations, because he is predominantly hyposensitive, he may still have his own hypersensitivities. He may need to have labels cut out of clothing; he may not be able to tolerate some laundry products; he may hate embroidery or other irregular surfaces on clothing, especially on the inside. He may refuse adhesive bandages. You may not be able to find a type of underpants he can stand to wear.

He may covet a satin edged blanket; he may love to pet your silk shirtsleeve; he may want fur textures all around him. Try to met these sensory needs extensively and appropriately.

If your Alfie is a hyposensitive child with autism who cannot show you sources of pain, perhaps his body awareness, including his perception of where pain comes from, is not focused. You can help him construct a more differentiated way to refer to himself.

A child who cannot easily point to or name the origin of pain and discomfort on his body can be made more specifically aware of location of sensation by having an adult touch spots he cannot easily see, such as the back of his neck, with a warm washcloth or an ice cube, while asking him to point to the spot where he feels the new sensation. Many practice sessions can help Alfie report problems more accurately, because you are increasing and localizing sensation for him to build a mental map of his body.

Another way to increase your Ruby's body awareness and provide reference points for the names of body parts is to make a life-sized cardboard replica of her. Trace her body while she is lying down, using any convenient corrugated cardboard or durable posterboard of suitable size. She might like to help, with the spots she can reach.

You can name Ruby's body parts as your marker passes by them, and later you can add a more realistic outline if you need to. If you have a digital photo of Ruby, print it as close to life size as possible and adhere it to the cardboard replica's face.

Cut out the arms separately from the body, and reattach with brass fasteners or cloth tape that allows you to move the arms. You can make joints in the elbows if you like. Think about folding the legs at the hip and knee for appropriate function, or cut across the knee joint and reattach with fabric tape so they bend.

You now have a paper doll of your own Ruby. Dress her in some of Ruby's outgrown clothes. These replicas can be electrifyingly lifelike.

Tip # 73b: Have your Aiden use sight to strengthen his body experience.

Try the "I See You" game. If your Aiden can talk, strengthen his body experience and help him become aware of others by having him face another child and take turns describing how each sees the other. If he signs, have him sign. Renaud says, "I see Aiden's brown hair," while Aiden may say, "I see Renaud's green eyes." You can vary this game by trying it with all the kids in the neighborhood, and all of your relatives. Some children with autism may not be able to deal with adjectives and nouns together, especially those adjectives concerning abstract concepts like colors. Help them make simpler comments if needed.

Building the self-concept through achievement

You have helped Ava build up her body awareness. But your Ava may still not experience herself as a capable person, and may even have learned in some circumstances to be, or to appear to be, helpless. So you will want Ava to increase her awareness of herself as a capable person who can get results in the world, who can accomplish things, even at an early age. You can help her build a robust concept of her efficacy in several ways:

Tip # 74: Narrate what Ava is doing. If you have a free hand, try to sign while you are narrating.

Why this works to build self-concept:

When a family member or carer tells Ava what she is doing while she is doing it, Ava has a chance not only to understand more spoken language but also to become self-conscious about her actions, whether she is petting the cat, throwing a ball, riding a scooter, climbing a tree, eating an apple, slamming the door, looking at a book, or stuffing a potato up your car's tailpipe.

When you observe, "Oliver is building with blocks," or, "Jessica is skipping," you increase the amount of spoken language your child understands, and in so doing, you increase your child's confidence and self-assurance.

Tip # 75: Keep a rich variety of toys, tools, and materials for Ava to play with.

She can, for example, fish for magnetic puzzle pieces in a dishpan using a little magnet on a string and tiny fishing "rod." (You can convert an ordinary puzzle piece by pushing a metal thumb tack into it.) She can thread large beads onto a shoelace; she can pour dry rice from little bottles into a larger container using a funnel. She can blow bubbles! You can wrap some items in tissues or aluminum foil to teach Ava to use those materials. You can seal some small puzzle pieces in a paper envelope, and show her how to cut it open with scissors. You can, if you are adventurous, put a small toy into a balloon, blow it up, and show Ava how to pop the balloon to get the toy. Your toys and materials do not have to be expensive.

Try to find some toys that lend themselves to symbolic play. Lincoln logs® and building construction toys are good examples. Ava can build a cabin with the Lincoln logs®, and let her doll live in it. You can race a toy dog into Ava's cabin, while you make barking noises. You could help her build a barn for a toy cow and horse.

Rotate toys so that when one loses its interest, you can store it temporarily and replace it with something different.

Tip # 76a: Create a can-do board showing your child's skills.

Remind your Ava of her skills and accomplishments by collecting photos of her as she roller skates, rides a horse, makes pizza. Even better if you make sure someone is narrating for her as you take the photos. You will enhance her positive self-image if you post these photos on Ava's can-do board, somewhere where she will easily and frequently see them—and so will everyone else! Label them too, to increase Ava's sight reading vocabulary.

If your family has access to a computer, and the Internet, you could create a family website showing Ava's abilities to an even wider audience.

If Ava has brothers and sisters, give a separate board to each child to display each one's accomplishments.

Every so often, take Ava to her board and point out some of your favorite photos, reminding her what she was doing. Compliment her.

If your board is large enough, you can consider showing sequences of photos, such as Ava helping groom the horse, Ava helping saddle the horse, Ava riding, Ava helping remove the saddle and fill the water container, Ava giving the horse a carrot.

Tip # 76b: If you see your Noah
spontaneously varying some of his routines
and skills on his own, help him expand them
even more. Narrate, photograph, and add
the new variations to the can-do board.

Perhaps your Noah loves the outdoor slide. He may suddenly
fly down the slide on his back, on his stomach, or sitting on
a bit of waxed paper he cleverly removed from the kitchen.
Applaud these developments and try to diversify them even
more as long as they are safe, because they show your Noah
is gaining increased awareness of his body, and greater
competence using his body.

If it is hot, you might want to position a hose at the top
of your little backyard slide, so Noah can zip down in the
water! If you can find a safe slide down into a pool, Noah
might be ecstatic! Not to mention a safe log plume ride…

One day your Benjamin may intensely desire to walk *up* a dry
slide, and climb down the steps on the other side. So what?
Let him, as long as you can prevent him from falling. That
trick requires some skill.

Tip # 77: Encourage and honor choices
your child with autism makes.

You develop your child's executive function, and her ability
to make her own decisions, when you encourage choices.
One way to enhance executive function is to "change your
mind" multiple times in the course of an activity, about the
direction you and your child may be walking, about which
fruit to put on the table, and after several changes of mind,
say to your child, "Oh, OK, OK, what do YOU want?"
Accept her choice.

Exercising the freedom to make choices also bolsters your child's sense of self. You can offer many simple choices to your child with autism, for example, choices of shoes and clothing, choices of snacks or favorite meals, preferred games, books, pets, and toys. Older children might be able to choose where to go play for an afternoon. Don't offer a choice if you really cannot honor all the options.

So let your William choose whether to wear a yellow or a blue shirt to school today. Let your Ben choose whether to wear his blue or his red toddler shoes, or one of each. Their happiness in their selections will be obvious, and their glowing faces will show enhanced self, even if they cannot yet speak!

Whenever your child makes a true choice, he builds his confidence that he has options and can exercise them.

Note:

If your Vera always picks the first or last option mentioned, it is unlikely to be a true choice. If your Matthew usually chooses to work or play with whatever is closest to his dominant hand, that also may not be a real choice among options, but just a decision rule to take the most convenient one, no matter which one he really wants. Vary the position of toys, crayons, clothing, and treats.

Some children are so afraid of making a mistake and so dread correction that they may fear making any choices at all. Try to approve and compliment the choices they make. If you must make some corrections with your error-phobic Reggie, in cases where error-free teaching is not working, use a friendly, neutral comment such as, "Try this one."

What not to do: working against self development

Tip # 78: Never use time outs.

Of all the activities that work against your child developing body or self-awareness and ability to interact with others, none is more noxious than "time outs" to control negative behavior. Even in the more subtle forms of "time out" such as, "If you don't want to play this game you can sit over there by yourself," your Great Aunt Harriet is demonstrating a mind-set focusing on control rather than on your child's need to develop self awareness.

Tip # 79: Children with autism find, "Look at me," "Talk to me," and "Use your words" almost universally confusing.

Trust us. Just don't.

Tip # 80: Watch out for inadvertent teaching.

"Time outs" are also pernicious because they may inadvertently teach your child to use aggression, self-injury, or other unacceptable behavior to communicate.

A child who is over-stimulated in a home or classroom where music is blaring, or many vigorous conversations are surging and ebbing around him simultaneously, may lash out in desperation at his high-decibel sensory overload and his growing auditory processing back-up. He is trying, and failing, to follow those conversations; he is trying, and failing, to cope with the sound.

This would be a good time to give him earphones, earplugs, or other ear protection, or if he likes his own music via earphones, hand it over. If all else fails, cover his ears.

If he punches someone, or frantically bites his own fingers, and an adult removes him from this jarring environment for a "time out" in a quiet place, he learns that he can relieve his painful sensory overload by hitting someone, or by hurting himself. Since our Fouad has been vulnerable to sensory overload throughout his life, and sensory overload is likely to be a frequent event, when we use "time outs" with Fouad we are inadvertently teaching him to rely on aggression and injury to solve sensory problems.

Parent's example:

In a local school, I have seen a five-year-old boy with autism launch himself head first into a heavy wooden door in a desperate attempt to escape from the cacophony of his peers' whacking rhythm sticks and tambourines together. His aide gave him a "time out," along with a reprimand. I have to presume this young man spent a lot of his school years in protective headgear.

Another parent's example:

Trying to teach my young son a different but still socially acceptable way to get heavy feedback, I showed him a little cha-cha dance step with a big hip bump.

Although I was not aware of it at the time, I was not over being angry with him (Why? For flushing my office key? For eating the cat's food?), so a cloud of annoyance and irritation still hung over our interaction and gave a hostile significance to what he learned. Your child also may be hyper-attentive to other people's emotional states, so beware.

What did my Simon learn? That when he was angry he could run through the house backwards and attempt to ram his would-be victims with his derrière.

I called this Simon's "street butt fighting."

It took a couple of years to go away, although it became funny to everyone including Simon.

Yet another example:

In an early intervention program, my son's teacher had the children comb through boxes of dry potting soil to find buried toy animals, pebbles, and shells.

This may have been intended to teach the children that interesting things lurk below ground, and in other places where you cannot see them, and that objects last for a while and do not cease to exist just because you no longer see them. But my child did not reach those generalizations, which required him to connect potting medium with actual earth, a step he had no obvious way to make, and required him to forget what had just been buried, so he could be surprised to see it re-emerge. Instead he learned he should root through potting soil wherever he found it, in case something appealing might be found. Staff were unhappy when they found him in the lobby digging among the roots of the rubber plants.

This is both an example of inadvertent teaching and inappropriate generalization. Observers often say that children with autism may fail to generalize what they know, but it may be more accurate in some cases to say that they do not know what the conventional boundaries of generalizations are.

Inadvertent teaching, with its sometimes comical and sometimes destructive consequences, is so widespread that we have asked for a summary of the matter from an expert therapist, Lynn Medley, with many years' experience with children with autism.

An insider's observations on inadvertent teaching[4]

If you have ever set out to teach anyone anything, you have probably encountered the hidden dangers of inadvertent teaching: the phenomenon of setting out to teach one thing and accidentally teaching another. Just recently, having taught a group of middle schoolers with ASD that bacteria cause smelliness in adolescent nooks and crannies, I was sure most of the students learned that it was a good idea to wash more thoroughly and more frequently. One student, though, was so intrigued that he began checking and comparing the odors of different cavities without regard to where he was or in whose company!

Inadvertent teaching occurs when the "teacher" (whoever is in this role, whether it be parent, sibling, actual teacher, classroom assistant, or therapist) fails to predict correctly which portion of their lesson will stand out to a pupil, how it will be interpreted, or how the portions will relate.

The classic behavioral example goes as follows: a parent and son go to the grocery store. Lincoln, the child with autism, is overwhelmed by the sights and sounds, by the restrictions, by not knowing how long this grocery trip might go on, by the fact that this was a change in the usual schedule, etc. When the experience gets to be too much, Lincoln covers his ears and shrieks shrilly. Negotiations don't work, so the

---

4   The authors thank Lynn Medley, M.S., C.C.C.-S.L.P., for contributing this section. Ms. Medley, Co-Director of Medley and Mesaric Therapy Associates, is a speech therapist in private practice in the eastern US. She specializes in communications and education, with a particular focus on apraxia in autism. In addition to her practice of private clients, she also consults with school districts and other educational organizations and provides advanced training workshops for teachers and therapists. Ms. Medley has been an expert witness in the area of language pathology, a consultant for the US Department of Education, and a speech therapist for some years at the Johns Hopkins Autism Clinic/Kennedy Krieger Institute Children's Center for Autism and Related Disorders in Baltimore, MD.

parent gives up and leaves a full cart of groceries to take Lincoln out of the store. We can't blame the parent, but we can be sure that Lincoln learned that a dependable way to avoid staying in the grocery store is to shriek.

This may be the classic behavioral example. But what about when you're trying to teach your child to say "Hi" to people, and every time she does, you respond by saying, "Good job!" so before long your child is saying, "Hi good job!" Inadvertent teaching.

Or when, in an effort to model urinating into the toilet, you show your child the water coming out of the garden hose and into a basin, only to find that your child now refuses to urinate anywhere except in the yard. Inadvertent teaching.

Maybe it was the time your speech therapist was working very hard on getting your child to look at her eyes in order to get information, and prompted him by saying, "Check in!" after which your child called out, "Chicken!" (what *he* heard when the therapist said, "Check in") every time he made eye contact. Inadvertent teaching.

Did you ever think your child would actually label colors with the names of race car drivers, according to the color of their cars? That he would believe that he could not read because he did not have glasses to don the way that he observes his parents and teacher do when they prepare to read?

Did you ever think that your child would be so clever as to make choices between two items on the table, given the command "Find the X," by reading the behavior specialist, choosing the item on the opposite side from the behavior specialist's hand that flinched ever so slightly in case it needed to block your child's reaching for the wrong answer? Inadvertent teaching.

How do you avoid these pitfalls? Here are a few tips:

Tip A: Know your audience. In a group of eight middle schoolers with ASD, there is bound to be one who is more interested in the bacteria than in the reactions of other people when he experiments with it. Perhaps he needs an individualized lesson.

Tip B: Walk a mile in the child's shoes, and walk that mile outside the box. What will this child's senses tell him? Will he hear "check in" or "chicken"? Will he focus on the fact that you put on glasses before you read, or on the direct instruction he gets every day at school?

Tip C: Retrace your steps. If a child does something you don't expect, do your best to figure out why. If he is able to answer, "Why did you do... ?" (as in, "Why did you shriek in the grocery store?"), ASK. If he is not able to answer "Why," see tip B. If and when you know "why," you can now return to tip A.

Tip D: When you are purposefully trying to teach something, watch what you do and say before and after. It is hard for children with autism to know what is the most relevant to you, and they easily make errors of choosing the wrong part on which to focus.

Tip E: Know, too, that a child will latch on to *anything* that might work, when you're teaching communication skills in particular, and she just doesn't know what you expect: the peeling edge of a picture symbol rather than the picture itself, the twitch of the adult's hand telling her which object not to choose, the other words in the sentence that give enough context that he doesn't have to know the target vocabulary word. You would too, but it doesn't mean you'd be able to use the skill in a different situation.

Tip F: Be specific (and particular) if you are going to use praise or inducements. Instead of praising peeing in the yard, save your big praise for the potty.

Tip G: Inadvertent teaching is the adult's mis-step, not the child's. Try, try again.

Tip H: Inadvertent teaching moments make great stories. When you realize what you've done, relax and have a good laugh about it. Share your stories with your friends—you can bet they'll have some, too.

More what not to do: working against self development

Tip # 81: Do not force your autistic child to remain sitting for lengthy periods.

We now know that some autistic children require motion to be able to sense their bodies, and to stimulate clear thinking and stay focused. So it will certainly be harmful to require such a child to stay seated for extended periods of time. An autistic child who requires massive sensory input will be starved for sensation if she is obliged to sit still for long. She will be tempted to bolt, or break something.

Instead, try to add sensory feedback to table work, and try to find furniture, toys, and art materials that give sensory input. Some children will benefit from using fidget toys they can keep in a pocket, or a small piece of soft fabric.

Relating strategies, examples of games, common activities, and shared chores

Tip # 82: Build your child's sense of family belonging, responsibility, and personal effectiveness by sharing chores.

Eventually, assign some chores solely to your child.

It makes good sense for your autistic child to have regular chores around the house, according to his growing interests and abilities. These responsibilities integrate him into the family and show that he is necessary.

You may need to stimulate your child's awareness that he is needed. You can show him in the garden, for example, by loading heavy rocks into a bucket and poking a pole through the handle. You pick up your side, and point to the other, signing and asking, "Help, Nathan?" Carry them to a reasonable spot and ask Nathan to help you unload them where they are needed.

If your Lily loves the dog, you can teach her to feed the dog and fill the dog's water bowl. It might add to the meaning if Lily eats and drinks something while the pet dog is eating and drinking; you point this out, and narrate it. Perhaps Lily can brush the dog, and then brush her hair.

Your Charlie can help clear the table after meals; your Riley can sort the silverware. Frank can help take out the trash; Celine can put the outgoing mail in the box. Emma might like to spray and wipe the windows.

Children with autism may enjoy helping wash the car, especially if it is conspicuously dirty. Sensory-craving kids may be happy to help break up sticks and branches in the garden, and carry recycling.

Visual or literate autistic children may benefit from a chores chart posted on the wall, showing in words, photos, or picture icons which jobs are theirs.

Yours, mine, and ours

When you are assigning chores, you may notice that your Maya needs some practice with "mine" and "yours" for smooth family relations.

One way to help Maya work out possession is to pile up all the shoes in the house and have Maya sort them. Sometimes intrude, take one of Maya's, and try, and conspicuously fail, to put in on your own foot, saying, "Mine? Oh no, not mine," or something similar. Have Maya practice signing and if possible saying, "Mine," as she gathers up her own shoes.

Tip # 83: Try a group building project.

Toy boat

Try building a toy boat with your child with autism. If she has brothers and sisters, they can help too.

The boat consists of three pieces—a hull, cabin, and mast—that your Charlotte can put together with some pegs, either precut or cut from dowel rods.

Parents, or other adults, can preshape the parts in advance. Using a 2 × 4 inch board, make the hull about eight inches long and four inches wide, tapering as you see fit. Make the cabin about four to five inches long and 2.5 inches wide. The mast can be a piece of 1/4 inch dowel rod about 8 inches high.

You will need a drill, a mallet, or a hammer, a vice or bench dogs on a workbench, and some waterproof paint and paintbrushes.

Pre-drill two 1/8 inch holes in the hull about half way through the wood. Also drill a 1/4 inch hole in the hull for the mast. Mark some corresponding spots on the underside of the cabin. Show your Charlotte how to open the vice on the workbench and hold the cabin securely. Help her drill out the holes all the way through.

When the holes are drilled, have Charlotte drop a straw or a pipe cleaner through the holes, to see what she has accomplished.

Next, place the hull and the cabin on a flat surface so Charlotte and the other kids, if any, can see that the pieces are separate. Align the holes in the cabin with the holes in the hull, and help Charlotte pound in the dowel rod bits or precut pegs. Perhaps Charlotte can pound one in, and her brother can pound in the other.

Show Charlotte and her brother that they have attached the two pieces. Hurray! Maybe someone else would like to pound in the mast.

Have the children pick some paint colors and paint the boat.

After it dries, pop it in the sink or tub to show its seaworthiness.

If you like, make a small triangular sail, and attach a small screw eye to the front of the boat so you can attach a ball of string to your boat. Take the children to a lake where you can wade, and launch their boat.

Bon voyage!

Unreliable furniture

If your Neil clings to his father and will not be pried away, you might try a building project with him.

Find a chair or two, and a small table that can be taken apart. Make sure they are a size suitable for your child.

While your Neil is watching, take the legs off the chair. Hand him a hammer, and help him pound the legs back in. Then encourage him to enjoy the fruits of his labors by sitting in the newly assembled chair. Repeat with the table: take the legs off, and have Neil help reattach them, with nuts and bolts, or by screwing them in like a light bulb, or hammering them, whatever the case may be. Have him pound on the table, and notice that it is sturdy.

Then, after an interval, perhaps the next day, while he is engaged in something else, remove a chair leg just before he sits in the chair. If he slips off, express shock and amazement! Hand him the hammer and ask him to fix it. While he is carefully hammering, loosen a table leg. When you ask Neil to do a little coloring on the table, watch it keel over. Give him the table leg and see if he can fix it by himself. If not, lend a hand.[5]

You can expand this exercise to anyone willing to cooperate: siblings, friends, and other relatives. Now Neil feels competent to repair furniture.

Tip # 84: Use illustrations to increase your child's appreciation of emotion on family members' and other people's faces.

It may take your Liam a while to create a mental face map that allows him to assign meaning to changes in face contours. While he is constructing this map, he won't be able to read family members' and other people's emotions from their faces very accurately.

If you think your Liam needs practice recognizing emotions on people's faces, so that he can respond, one option is to use photographs, pre-printed cards, or printed images from web clip art.

Another option is to use a cooperative adult or convivial child to make corresponding faces, and narrate, "OOOO, look, Auntie Julie is MAD! See Colin? He is happy! Hey, Grandfather is surprised! Look, Auntie Tril is making a monster face!"

---

5   To avoid inadvertently teaching your child that his repairs are faulty, wait for a bit before testing them. After all, objects to break over time.

If you have good printed images, put a few in front of your Liam and practice having him identify them when you ask, "Liam, show me the laughing baby! Give me the sad lady. Where is the mad little boy? Is this guy scared?"

Tip # 85a: Use music to intensify meaning and enhance relevance at home.

Music, both lyrics and melody, offers powerful tools to reach your child with autism. Lyrics need to be as concrete as possible, as based in your autistic child's immediate experience as possible.

Melody need not be restricted at all.

Music can also convey meaning for your autistic children when other forms of communication fail. You can use particular songs tailored to your current purposes, to add information. When you are traveling, a song can remind your Nathan of your destination. One song accompanies you to the grocery store, another to the doctor, a third to the park. Try to work in some specifics, such as the names of the people you will see, or what you will do when you arrive. The lyrics convey meaning, while the melody provides continuity— since it extends over time—and it gives reminders of other trips. So songs reduce anxiety.

Music is reassuring and engaging, it can be informative, and some kids can join in singing, clapping, humming, or tapping on the window in rhythm. If you play your Charlotte's favorite music while you travel, it also communicates to her that you care about her tastes and choices.

If your Ben prefers Otis Redding while he is in pre-school and can't possibly understand the lyrics, it won't hurt him. Play it anyway.

Continuous melody by itself can help establish continuity for your Oliver, who needs to construct his own reality one piece at a time. He will find it soothing and may want to play a tape, a CD or DVD, the radio, or other music source every waking hour. If this interferes with family life, try to teach him to use a device compatible with earphones. Try to accustom him to using the earphones by himself, without assistance. If you succeed, this skill can help him cope in public all of his life.

Examples of songs for your young child which family members can make concrete and immediately relevant:

"Old MacDonald." Since this song names animals typically found on farms in the USA, and imitates their sounds, its meanings are straightforward. However, our children tend to be quite visual and have difficulty integrating what they hear with what they see. So it would help your child connect the animal sounds to the animals themselves if you offer them pictures, plastic toy animals, or realistic stuffed animals *while* the child simulates the sounds the animals made. Then, a visit to a real farm where they could see the actual animals would be helpful and fun. That way the name of the animal, the sound it makes and what it looks like become firmly established.

"The Old Lady Who Swallowed a Fly." This song is frankly silly, with impossible verses such as, "I know an old lady who swallowed a horse," and so should generate some laughter, especially if you sing, sign, and over-act. These days you can find a set of toys to act out every verse.

"Eentsy Weensy Spider." This charming song about a hapless spider who went up the water spout has potential, if the event is acted out with several props. Try a toy spider, perhaps on a plastic thread, appearing to climb up a transparent water spout until the "rains" come and an adult pours water (rain) down the spout and washes the spider out.

An enactment makes the meaning clear to your literal-minded ASD child. Without that kind of demonstration we doubt that the child fully understands what a spout is or what the song is about.

After you have fun with the song, you can show the child some photos, slides, videos, or other imagery of spiders in their natural habitats. If that maintains interest, you could also consider showing the child how gutters and downspouts work the next time it rains on your house.

If you succeed beyond all measure with these "evidence-based" songs, you can try your own variations. Here is one parent's:

"Old Lorraine."

The itsy bitsy spider went up the water spout.

Down came Lorraine (from upstairs, or up the hill, or up the street) and washed the spider out.

Out came the sun and dried up old Lorraine

And the itsy bitsy spider went up the spout again.

This one may have more resonance if your neighborhood features a grouchy old lady.

"Ring Around the Rosy." Dr. Miller has noted that this song goes back to the Middle Ages, with unfortunate references. The ashes refer to the marking of houses with ashes if a plague victim had perished inside. "All fall down!" refers to the people falling down and dying of the plague.

However, the melody is simple, appealing, and you can certainly change the lyrics! Perhaps you could put the child in the center of the circle and sing, "Walk around our Joey/ Then we'll hear a story/Jump! Jump! Jump!/ We all fall down!" For variety, use other gaits the child enjoys, such as crawling, hopping, dancing and skipping, and let other family members take turns in the center, changing the lyrics to accommodate their names.

One parent whose household always harbored at least two or three cats composed a verse for this same melody, very much in her son's experience, that he would hear with interest and obvious engagement:

Cats are in the meadow

Eating buttercups

Hairballs, hairballs

They all throw up!

Sound effects can be provided.

"The Hokey Pokey Song." This song is excellent for body awareness, teaching left and right, awareness of prepositional relations, and just plain fun. It can readily be applied and expanded by having the child perform these actions in everyday situations. Put your right foot in the bath tub, put your left hand in the fountain water, etc. Dr. Miller strongly recommended this song as a basis for exercises for children on the spectrum.

"The Wheels on the Bus." This song has excellent potential if accompanied by visual images of a toy bus showing the wheels going round and round, and if parents or grandparents help the child act out the other parts of the song, while it is being sung. If you have a carton left from a large appliance such as a refrigerator, you could use the box to build a large cardboard bus with wheels that go round, wipers that can go "swish, swish" and a driver who sends people to the back of the bus. Experience with the physical props that correspond to the song would do much to generalize the song meanings to real world bus experiences. A real bus ride would be great too!

General Principle. *Choose songs that relate to your child's everyday life and interests. Concretize the songs so that what they hear and what they see—and, when possible, what they touch—coincide. Have them act out parts of the songs. When you make the meanings concrete, visible, audible, touchable, and imitable, not only are you accenting the meaning of the song, you also making it far more likely that your child will generalize the song meanings to real life situations.*

Tip # 85b: Make up your own variations of common songs, and original songs based in your mutual, immediate experience. Sing them while you are doing whatever the song is about.

One parent tells us:

> When your Jaime is at the age of exploration and is taking out all the canned goods in the kitchen, help him make a train with them. As he opens all the cabinet doors to look in, getting in your way, you may be able to cope better if you sing "Let My Love Open the Drawers…to Your Heart," kudos to Pete Townsend.

Another parent reports:

> My son loved to sit on the curb, in our rather clean and fresh rural neighborhood, after a storm to play in the gutter in the rushing water. This led to our "Dirt Song." Our neighbors know all the verses.

"The Dirt Song."

You got dirt, dirt, dirt

On your shirt, shirt, shirt.

You got sand, sand, sand

In your hand, hand, hand.

You got rocks, rocks, rocks

In your socks, socks, socks.

We got mud, mud, mud

In our blood, blood, blood.

Chorus:

We love sand and mud and worms.

We squish dirt and laugh at germs.

We love dirt!

Note that repetition helps some apraxic kids speak.

Intermezzo

More on the nature of family ties: the family DVD collection

You may think you know the laws of probability. You may, for example, have advanced degrees, be an actuary, an insurance adjustor, or a mathematician, or just have suffered through statistics in college. So figure this one out.

Your Graham is insisting on playing a DVD. Immediately! He can't wait. The universe will end, a tantrum will ensue which will rock the foundations, hurry and put in the DVD you have in your hand. OK, it has no label. But how bad could it be? You wonder. We only HAVE *Barney*, wildlife DVDs, *Winged Migration*, Disney, *Finding Nemo*, the *Deadliest Catch* crab fishing series, and *Monkeys*.

So you put it in and push the play button. It will be fine.

But what it is, is the torture scene from *The Battle of Algiers*.

9

A FEW MORE TIPS FOR PARENTS

Establishing connections and emotional bonds

We must remind you: your beloved child's autism is not your fault. Remember that your Riley's apparently unresponsive behavior is a part of her condition, it is not a personal rejection of *you*. An abiding and deep relationship may be there although she cannot show you in the usual ways without help. And you will help her.

Tip # 86a: Be aware that there is often a bond between parent and child even if you do not detect it. Your child may cherish you even though she keeps this strong tie to herself.

Look for it!

Example:

One parent reports that her Amy seldom hugged her, often looked away, had to be taught how to kiss, and did not often come to her for help. But once, when the mother did not beat the school bus home, she found her Amy trudging wearily from room to room, searching for her mother in all the accustomed places, evidently abandoned, bereaved, and weeping bitterly. Amy's mother knew that Amy loved her and missed her.

Your child's love may show up disguised, as jealousy or anger, or may appear indirectly in other ways that may be hard to recognize.

Example:

Dr. Miller recounted many occasions in which parents with a new baby to care for suddenly find their child with autism distressed, anxious, aggressive, or even self-injuring. Here, like everyone else, children with autism are revealing their craving for more attention when attention has to be divided with the baby. That is, they are revealing that they love you and need you.

You may find that your child Jaime hits you "for no reason" if you attend to your baby when Jaime craves your attention. You may deal with this most successfully by increasing communication with him, saying for example, "Mom is changing Angela's diaper now. Next, Mom will play with Jamie," and by trying to keep one hand on him, to tousle his hair, or pat his shoulder, as you turn to your other child.

It is natural to withdraw if you feel your ASD child's odd behavior as rejection, or to want to isolate your autistic child and to turn more attention to a baby or a typical child. But your autistic child needs you intensely, and needs your emotional support and availability even more than a typical child.[1]

---

1   Just a reminder that *you* need respite. Do everything possible to get some help. Local schools and colleges may be prospects for students who need internship credits or are looking for experience in special education. Nannies and student teachers are excellent catches.

But what if your child genuinely seems to have no bond with you?

Tip # 86b: You can build and strengthen a bond with your ASD child by maintaining a vigorous, supportive, playful, carefully instructive, and moderately challenging attitude in frequent interactions.

Build a bond, and your child's capacities, by maintaining your high demand/high support attitude. Interact often, with high expectations. Let your Michael dress himself and tie his own shoes, even if it takes longer. Help only as required. Let Sophie push the grocery cart instead of riding. Let Andrew try his own drawing and painting instead of showing him hand-over-hand, even if it is messier. He can help you clean up later.

Attitudes that work against establishing and maintaining emotional bonds, and which may delay your child's advancement

- Making demands which make no sense to your child, such as trying to teach the names of the days of the week and seasons of the year when you are not certain your Jayden knows what a day is.

- Giving up on your Mia and doing everything for her or with her hand-over-hand, so she has scant opportunity to exercise her own skills, and learns to be helpless.

- Leaving your Rahul in front of the TV or a computer screen all day because he likes it.

Not all TV is noxious; Sesame Street and similar programs with interactive elements are constructive for younger children, especially if your Rahul watches them with his friends, who comment and participate. But be cautious about murder mysteries, horror films, monster movies, invading space aliens, and similar genres, since your child with autism may have difficulty knowing that these plots and images are fiction. You do not want to flood his consciousness with violent images that will alarm him during the day and generate nightmares in the evening. Remember he may have little gating function and probably experiences most incoming sensations including video personally, immediately, and consciously, as though they were real and perhaps as though he were involved.

Tip # 87: If your child avoids eye contact and often glances sideways to look at objects, consult your physician or nutritionist.

This may be a condition which can be cleared up with vitamin A in cod liver or other natural sources.

But if it isn't, help your Lily learn to look at you by involving yourself in her favorite routines. Suppose she loves to color with crayons. When she has only one crayon, slip it out of her hand and hold it in front of your face, preferably at her eye level. As she reaches for the crayon, she inevitably looks at you as well. Give her the crayon right away, and repeat this many times; try it with other routines and other objects. Soon your Lily will look at you more comfortably.

Why this works:

This little trick, over time, establishes your importance to Lily. First she sees you as background to her crayon; then, as she takes the crayon, you come into clear focus as the relevant central figure in her life that you are.

Tip # 88a: If your child has a tendency to disappear into his own world, combat this disappearance by "getting in his face."

Some harmless ways to recapture your Ariel instead of letting her slip away: carefully annoy your Ariel. Slip her shirt half on so she must wiggle around to find where to put her arms. Put one sock on your Jessica and hold on to the other one, absent-mindedly. Step in front of your Cameron as he tries to walk by, bump into your Grace as she steps around the corner.

If your Jake ignores all the toys you try to interest him in, tuck one or two into his pockets or under his shirt, next to his skin. The extra sensation will help Jake relate, and may amuse him.

Tip # 88b: If your Zoe tends to withdraw, enhance and enrich her reality to help her engage with it and with you.

You can enhance and enrich your child's reality in many ways. One way is to elevate your height-seeking Zoe, on the Elevated Square structure described in *The Miller Method®* (2007, pp. 90–93); in a tree house, on a raised picnic table bench, a run of sawed-off logs, or any safe structure that will support Zoe's weight at about 30 inches off the ground. In each case, you are enhancing her experience of height and reducing her opportunities to fly off in all directions, requiring her to pay close attention to foot position, balance, and use of hands, so that her focus is enhanced.

You may also want to deploy toys that stimulate many senses, such as tuning forks and toys that vibrate while making a sound, flashing light toys (probably not red if your child has a seizure disorder), or a lightbox you can use as a play surface, textured toys, bristly and soft; moving toys, and chimes or mobiles to hang from the ceiling.

More on enhanced and enriched realities
Why you might want a dog

If your neighborhood, home owners' association, or local culture allow it, a kid-friendly dog not only may track your Ben in an emergency, he can also help teach your child to take turns, to interact, and to remain calm. The dog can be a playmate and surrogate brother. Fetching a tossed ball is only one game suitable for a dog and a child with autism. Tug-of-war with a soft cotton rope is another excellent choice: the dog will enjoy it and your child will get the body stimulation he needs.

A standard issue dog may be exactly what you need. Specially trained service dogs for young people with autism can be life-changing, although the dogs are only available in small numbers. Dogs can increase autistic children's ability to show affection and remain responsive to other people. Some autistic youngsters who cannot otherwise appear in public maintain their composure when they are with their dogs. Some children have learned to talk while playing with their dogs. To find more information, see service dog websites in your country such as http://autismservicedogsofamerica. com and http://.4pawsforability.org in the USA, www.nsd. on.ca in Canada, and www.righteouspups.org.au in Australia.

What to do for those repetitive activities ("perseverative behavior"), unacceptable conduct, and aborted communication attempts
These may capture your child, drive you nuts, and interfere with clear communication and normal interaction.

For sensory or physiological reasons, your ASD child Alexander may be drawn into long periods of repetitive and apparently pointless activity which may be not only annoying to you and to others, but which also keep Alex closed in on himself. You can transform these routines into flexible, interactive activities which help Alex communicate with other people. In each case, your goal is to make the routine interactive, to expand it to another person, to add flexibility to Alexander's routines, and to increase his sense of capability. Here are some examples, and variations, of ways to cope with perseveration, unacceptable public conduct, and other problems common to families with ASD children.

Biting

Do check for problems with erupting teeth, cavities, chipped, or broken teeth, in case biting is a sign of a local problem. But if it is more than that, try a massive increase in oral stimulation. For a very small child, consider using a pacifier. For an older child, find an array of items and devices your child can bite on for sensory input to the jaw, for relief of tension, and for handling pain he may not be able to tell you about. These might be stiff, flexible, or crunchy items which are edible or only chewable. Plastic tubing in long pieces, hard chewing gum, popcorn, rubber toys originally made for dogs, speech therapy devices meant for use inside the mouth, and all-day sucker taffy are some options for resourceful parents. Watch for and throw away anything that could disintegrate into pieces suitable for choking on. Find some items that are easy to transport, or that your child can carry in her pocket for use as needed.

Dropping or throwing objects

Your Alex may throw or drop objects because he has not completed the normal experiments all children go through as youngsters, tossing objects off their highchair trays, out the car windows, over the porch railing, down the well, etc. You can help Alex finish this bit of intellectual development by a thorough exploration of throwing.

Tip # 89: To gain control over dropping and throwing, practice throwing and dropping with your child in contained circumstances.

Teach him how to vary and expand his routine, and come to share it with you and others.

Example:

Sit on the floor with your Alex, and put next to him a large basket full of plastic balls. If throwing captures him, Alex will start tossing the balls right away. Point in different directions to guide his throwing. If he accepts your suggestions and communication, try encouraging Alex to target balls to different containers. Throw one in a clean garbage can, to show him how it sounds, or toss one into a bucket of water to hear the splash. If his aim is good, encourage him to throw some through a wooden target with holes in it, or throw some at a hanging object such as a metal triangle, a bell, or a plastic toy on a spring. As Alex gets involved with the targets, move and rearrange them.

When he has noticed the new arrangement, have him drop balls of several different sizes into the garbage can, and then into the bucket.

If Alex continues to be able to work with you, now start taking turns throwing WITH him. You may need to hold his arm while you throw, for the first few times. When he waits for you to take a turn, you know that he understands turn taking. Now his throwing is interactive!

Narrate each step as you do it.

Some parents find it helpful to refer to themselves and their child in the third person because it may be simpler to follow: "Frank throws! Now Dad throws!" rather than, "You throw! Now I will." (To a new language learner, it may seem that everyone is "you" and everyone is "I" at different times, for impenetrable reasons.)

You might want to set up a special time every day to throw balls, toys, etc. Remember to stop while your child is still interested.

If your Alex knows numbers, you may find it helpful to count as you throw with your Alex. When you are ready to stop, you could count down,"Three, (throw), two (throw), one (throw), all finished." If Alex understands concepts like "how many," you could ask him, "How many more times shall we throw?" and keep track, preferably on a board he can see.

If you take five or ten minutes a day to throw with Alex, he will gradually find that he has finished his experimentation in this field. It's even better if you can gradually develop throwing into a game of catch, or a game of fetch with the dog. Teach your dog the "fetch" command, spoken and signed, so even your nonverbal child can play.

Flapping

Your Carter may flap his hands and arms vigorously for the same reason two- or three-year-olds might: he is giving himself information about his body position in space, when he doesn't feel it adequately standing or sitting still.

Tip # 90a: For flapping, anything you do to flood your child with physical sensation will help.

Examples:

Heavy input occupational therapy, rough-housing, and massage and compressions may help.

If your flapping Zoe is small enough, tossing her in the air and letting her fall onto a bed or soft sofa may also help.

Talk to your doctor or nutritionist about whether vitamin A in a natural form like cod liver oil could help neurological input be felt more strongly. (See the work of Dr. Mary N. Megson (2000).)

Tip # 90b: If your Gavin flaps his hands often, but does not seem to need more large-scale sensations, you can teach him to flip a pen or a pencil back and forth in his fingers, or use a fidget toy instead.

Tip # 90c: For flapping, try to increase your Alex's awareness of his body by having him crash cymbals together with his hands.

Why this helps:

It is fun, and it provides multiple sorts of sensory stimulation that raise body awareness. Alex will most likely be thrilled with the vibrant and complex sound he has caused, heard, and furthermore, felt, as he banged the cymbals together.

Variations:

Offer your Alex sandpaper bars for each hand, finger cymbals for many fingers, a band of bells to wear on each wrist, rhythm sticks to bang together, cowbells, or any other noise- or music-maker to be used with both hands.

You can also try giving your Alex a tambourine to bang on; one with bells or jingling disks around the rim is even better.

Flushing

Continual toilet flushing can be intensely satisfying to your ASD child. Your Eli may love the whooshing sound as the water empties out of the tank; he may love to watch the spiraling water drain down into the pipes, and he may find it delightful that some objects can be made to disappear by following the swirling water. He may feel compelled to continue. He may have in mind a series of experiments in specific gravity.

Potty flushing can be a powerful routine to disrupt. So rather than simply ordering him to stop…

Tip # 91: If your Eli is a repetitive flusher, first make the flushing interactive. Then develop some spin-off routines that will attract Eli, and make those interactive as well. Finally, alternate spin-offs with flushing until the drive to flush subsides.

Interactivity is the easy part. Take turns flushing with your Eli, narrating as you do so, saying, "Eli flushes!" "Now Grandmother flushes!" etc.

Then devise your spin-offs. These spin-offs need to be little causal routines that capture the sense of motion and perhaps sound and sparkle, and use water to attract Eli. If Eli feels strongly compelled to flush repetitively, he may need experience with several other spin-offs before he can resist the impulse to flush, and his attraction to flushing will fade.

*Examples of water-based spinoffs
that Eli may find alluring:*

Take turns operating a drinking fountain, narrating, "Eli pushes the button! Look at the water!" or, "Aunt Carrie pushes!" or, "Splash, splash, splash!" etc.

Take turns spraying with a hose in your backyard, yelling, "Eli sprays! Then Uncle Frank sprays!"

Take turns pouring water over a toy water wheel, narrating, "Eli pours! Now Susan pours!"

For some children, the sound component of flushing may be compelling by itself. For these kids, you can take turns "flushing" a toy toilet by pushing the sound button as another type of spin-off, or take turns pushing the play button on a tape recorder with a pre-recorded flush.

Try to get Eli to tolerate more than one spin-off before you go back to interactive flushing. With practice, build in more and more spin-offs before returning to flushing. Over time, the more acceptable routines will gradually drain flushing of much of its power and Eli will lose interest.[2] We hope this happens before your water bill skyrockets.

Hitting

Try to turn attempts at hitting into communicative physical contact, such as high fives, handshakes, or patty-cake games if your child is small. Try to maximize physical contact over the course of the day, and encourage contact sports and frequent physical activity for larger children.

If hitting is a persistent problem, try dramatic sensory responses such as blowing on a lifeguard whistle, dropping

---

2　A partial list of things consigned to a watery grave at our house includes: a spring toy Slinky, a wooden Jacob's ladder toy, toothbrushes and bars of soap, dog bones, pairs of socks, an entire box of tissues, and a toy goldfinch that sang when you walked by.

a blanket over your child, pouring a quart of water over his head, or surrounding him suddenly with a cloud of soap bubbles generated with a battery-powered bubble blower. (See Chapter 5 for a few more comments.)

Kicking

If kicking has become a problem with a small child, try to deal with it by holding your child's hands, staying out of range as much as possible, and repeating positively, "Next, we are going to… " (whatever is on your schedule). Then move on smoothly to that activity.

Note here that you are trying to convey the attitude that kicking does not accomplish anything, and doesn't mean much. In this version, you don't even bother saying, "No kicking."

If it is too late for that, you may need special equipment. One parent reports that she inadvertently taught her son that kicking is fun, dramatic, and a big thrill for all concerned, because the first time he kicked her, she did not see it coming, and, caught off-balance, she fell down, which was deeply rewarding to her small son (see "Watch out for inadvertent teaching," in Chapter 8). She got rid of kicking only by wearing hockey shin guards for six weeks, while moving on smoothly to the next activity.

Light flicking, light sensitivity, and sensitivity to fluorescent bulbs

If your Amelia likes to flip your light switches off and on, or repeatedly turn the TV monitor or a computer off and on, you can capture this annoying routine and transform it.

Tip # 92: When Amelia is flicking the lights or controls off and on, first turn the lights on and off with her, taking turns and narrating. Then substitute something similar, such as a flashlight, and take turns switching it on and off with her, still narrating.

Other examples:

You can also try substituting other cause and effect toys with switches, such as the light-up spinners and yo-yos, as well as more complicated flashlights such as ones with red filters, or multiple colors. Some science toy stores sell a flashlight that is powered by friction rather than a battery; you squeeze the trigger to generate light. These toys can add more tactile and visual interest than a flashlight alone and may make sounds which are attractive to your child.

Lining things up

Lining things up is a basic way to restore order in a confusing world. If your Liam is heavily involved in lining up objects to the exclusion of much else, you can use his desire to line up things to draw him out and make him more open to information.

Here are some steps to try if Liam is lining up little toy cars from his collection.

Tip # 93a: Become a car supplier (or a dealer in whatever he is organizing, such as wooden blocks or toy animals).

Here is the technique:

First, gather up for your own use a large number of little toy cars like the ones Liam is arranging.

Hand him one. If he takes it, good! If not, place it near the end of his trail of cars. If he doesn't pick it up, move it a bit closer, until he does.

After he has added a few of your cars to his line, hold the next one up next to your face so that he sees you as he takes it. You have just been added to the car lining-up routine!

Then, gradually move farther away from him, a foot or so at a time, so that he has to travel a bit to get the next car.

If Liam finds the distance distressing, come closer again.

When you succeed with this technique, you have expanded Liam's lining up, making it interactive and flexible, and you have introduced yourself into his play.

If that works, try to join him.

Try expanding the car play by driving your own toy car up and down beside Liam's car parade, or by trotting out a toy pony to jump over it.

Take a close look at Liam's car line when he is finished. Is it in some order, such as by color matching, car model, or number painted on the cars? If so, take note; he is showing you some categories in his thinking.

Tip # 93b: Try to join your Laila in her routine, to increase communication.

If your Laila is lining up blocks from a supply of her own, get some similar ones for yourself.

Try adding one of your blocks to her line. She may not be able to accept this! Perhaps she has her own plan, to organize them by shape or color, for example. Perhaps she simply cannot accept an expansion as large as your full participation.

But if she does accept your block, hurray! Try taking turns adding them. If one or two more of yours are accepted, the next time you add one, line it up slightly askew.

If Laila jumps up to come and straighten out your error, let her do that. Next time, again misalign the block you add, then look at your Laila as she is starting to become concerned, and quickly adjust the block. Nod knowingly, as if you have just become aware of her uneasiness. Repeat this process, each time making a different "error," and being careful not to stretch your Laila's tolerance of disorder too far. Remember to stop while she is still interested.

Block play can be expanded in other ways as well. You can try parallel rows of blocks, one for each of you. When a suitable length has been reached, you can try walking your fingers along the tops of your blocks, and then try to walk along Laila's as well. Encourage her to walk her fingers on your blocks.

You can try galloping a toy horse over your blocks, or jumping the blocks; see if your Laila will do the same. You can try driving a toy car along the blocks, making enthusiastic car noises; see whether Laila might try it as well. Try landing a toy plane there.

If you are using your blocks as a road for your toy cars, connect your two rows and try to drive on Laila's road. See if she will drive on yours.

If you think Laila is resilient enough, create a traffic jam; make honking noises; wipe your brow and exclaim, "Oh NO! I'm going to be stuck for hours!"

Don't be surprised if your child wants to crash the cars.

Other variations:

Add a ramp at the end of the block road and zoom some cars down it. Ask Laila to zip her cars down the ramp. Set up an imaginary gas station and refill the car tanks.

Try to extend this sort of play for 20–30 minutes every day, until the lining up ritual seems to lose gale force.

Tip # 93c: Try parallel play.

If your Sawyer is perturbed because you have disordered his row of farm animals, set up a row of your own beside his.

Then, as you add to your row, offer a toy animal to Sawyer. After he has accepted several, ask for one from him for your lineup. You can make this request vivid by signing "give" and tapping the palm of your open hand.

If he hands you an animal in return, you are on your way to establishing reciprocity.

Try to continue giving and receiving animals.

Masturbating or getting an enormous erection in public, or at home

Tip # 94: Carry a coat.

If your Max is masturbating in public, give him something bulky to carry, or have him push a shopping cart. If your Liam is overcome with love for the beautiful lady at the bakery, and shows it with a huge erection, try to prevent him from showing her, and try the same tactic of having him carry something bulky or push a shopping cart. Here, by your actions you are letting your child know that this is not a public sport, and you are offering him something else to do with his hands. If you don't have anything bulky enough, perhaps Liam could carry your coat. You want something to occupy his hands and obscure his enthusiasm.

And of course, if he comes to you for help with an erection he finds irritating, take him calmly to the bathroom and give him a cool wet washcloth to apply.

If you find your child with autism masturbating at home, you might just reorient her to her bedroom, leave her alone for five or ten minutes, and then knock and suggest something else to do.

Try to remain serene if you observe these entirely normal developments. If you are scandalized, and draw massive attention to masturbating, you can guarantee you will see a lot of it.

Nakedness: a related sensory issue

Tip # 95: Carry replacement clothing. And don't roll the car windows down much.

Perhaps you have a little MINK (multiple intensive needs kid) who loves the feel of wind, sand, water, or in fact almost anything flowing, blowing, or of textural interest, on his skin. So, to satisfy his intense hunger for these sensations, he will be buck-naked as much as possible.

If your child is verbal, you may try to explain when nakedness is acceptable, or that some people think it is not nice. Most likely he will stare at you in amazement and contradict you.

So you must be prepared. Your Owen will strip when you are looking, when you are not looking, when company is sitting down to eat, when the minister is at the door, and even when it would not possibly occur to you and you find it hard to believe as you are looking at it, e.g., in snow.

One parent reports that her son liked to strip before he crossed the street, to inquire about a dip in the neighbor's pool. Sometimes she could catch him, because he would stop to stick his finger up the statuary bear's nose. If she was not swifter than he, he would reach the neighbor's doorbell, often at five in the morning, attired only in a winning smile.

So you must anticipate that your Gabriel, Houdini-like, may suddenly remove his clothing:

- in the car, in the seatbelt, without getting out of the seatbelt (keep car windows closed)

- on the bus on the way to school

- at a store

- always, in the back yard, to get the full, juicy satisfaction of the wading pool.

And he may also dispose of his clothing, rapidly and efficiently, while you are not looking.

Out you go, for example, into the back garden, and there not only is your darling Nicolas attired solely in his birthday suit, but his other suit of clothes has disappeared off the face of the planet. They are not nearby, they are not near the garden hose, they are not by the back door, they are not hanging on the hook specially installed on the fence for this purpose; the dog is not wearing them, no other children have them; they are gone.

Possible solutions:

- They are in the fish pond.
- They are in the playhouse under the bed. Or in the bed, dripping.
- They have been lobbed over the six-foot plank fence and now repose on the other side, possibly in the neighbor's flowerbed, dog kennel, or garbage tip.

Be prepared for the possibility that this clothes peeling event may take place at a public wading pool, in which case the clothes may have been pitched into a nearby river, ditch, trash truck, the ocean, or other destination from which they cannot or should not be recovered.

Coping strategies:

Your instructions may fail to dissuade your sensory-hungry MINK for a long time. Meanwhile, consider some options:

- Carry an extra large cotton T shirt with you at all times. They fold up small and will cover your Owen, Nicholas, or Gabriel when all else fails.

- If you are traveling by car, never be without a couple of changes of clothes, perhaps his and yours, in the car. Sweatpants may be a good bet.

- For swimming, consider a one-piece zip front surf suit for your MINK, that fits close to the body and feels like skin. He may like to leave that one on.

- If you don't have the stamina to join a naturalist beach club where they won't object to your au naturel Gabriel, consider bike shorts, other compression clothing, or fun textured pants for him. If possible, let him help pick them out.

Opening and closing doors

If your Aubrey repeatedly opens and closes your doors, possibly enjoying giving them a good loud slam, you will probably find this tedious and want to change it.

Tip # 96a: If your Aubrey feels driven to open and close doors, you can playfully transform this routine by making it interactive.

Here is one way:

Narrate what your child is doing: "Aubrey is opening the door; Aubrey is closing the door," then join her. "Auntie Stella and Aubrey are opening the door! And closing the door!" Take turns. This often takes a lot of interest out of repeated door opening.

Tip # 96b: Expand this interactive opening and closing by making it into a game. Peek-a-boo is a good choice.

Stand on one side of the door, while Aubrey stands on the other. As Aubrey throws open the door, tap your chest and announce, "Here is Auntie Stella!" Then, as you open the door and spy your Aubrey, pat her on the chest and declare "There is Aubrey!"

Try this routine with other doors, and other people, until Aubrey begins to expect a person behind each door. Try it with shutters, curtains, and blinds. Show Aubrey, similarly, taking turns, how to open jars, storage containers, and boxes. You might want to prepare in advance by putting something interesting in each container you use.

Pinching

If your Sophie cannot talk yet, she may resort to frequent pinching or scratching as a way to create interaction with you. You will naturally want a more interesting substitute for the "Pinch Daddy 'til he bleeds" or "Hold Auntie Nicky's wrist and set your fingernails in it" game that may captivate your Sophie.

Note that if she has a high pain tolerance herself or if she seeks out pinching forces on her own body, it may be difficult to convince her that pinching hurts other people.

Tip # 97a: For pinching try "Sleeping Monster."

As soon as you think Sophie is about to pinch her father, have him pretend to fall asleep, snoring loudly. Coach Sophie to sneak up on him quietly, and try to touch him without waking him—i.e., NOT pinching! As Daddy hears Sophie approach, he roars to life and tries to grab Sophie!

Repeat this cycle as often as is convenient with an adult coaching Sophie about how to be stealthy and touch delicately. This intervention over time should help Sophie come to recognize play and gentle touch as a better way to make contact.

Tip # 97b: Another option to reduce pinching is "Move the Mountain."

If your Emma is a robust girl and loves heavy input, when she seems ready to pinch or claw, try a pushing game. Stand facing her and push your flat hands against hers to try to force your Emma (gently, of course) to back up. This works best if a third person can help organize the game, lining the two of you up, counting, "One, two, three, go!" and acting as a referee, saying, "Stop," or, "You win!" when someone succeeds in pushing the mountain back.

Rocking

If your Taylor needs a great deal of comfort and sensory information, she may only feel at ease while rocking when sitting or standing. She may seem unaware of anyone and everything else.

You can use her need to rock to reach into her world and bring her into communication with you.

Tip # 98: To reach your encapsulated rocking child, rock her yourself, gradually building up the rhythm of rocking, until you stop!

Try this:

In a comfortable rocking chair, or any other piece of furniture you think suitable, sit and position your Taylor astride one or both of your legs. Holding her back and neck securely and fondly, as you would any small child, look smiling into her face and slowly start rocking with her. Gradually increase the arc of the rocking, so that you go further backward and forward each time. Speed up slowly, consistent with safety. Then, when you are feeling the tempo yourself, and you think your Taylor is starting to anticipate the rocking motion, stop in mid-rock, when you are sitting upright.

The abrupt end to rocking begs for a response. If Taylor makes eye contact, or rocks a bit herself to show you what to do, and you answer by resuming rocking, she is already communicating with you about the need for more rocking.

Try to repeat this rocking exchange for 10 to 12 times. Be sure to stop while your child is still interested in more.

As Taylor becomes more conscious of her own body and her ability to communicate, you can use this opportunity to teach her the "more" or "rock" sign.

Variation with small children: horsey ride

Some small children who crave rocking motion will also enjoy sitting on an adult's knee while the adult bounces them, imitating the gait of a horse. You can hold both of your child's hands while you do this, and look into her face. Narration, sound effects, and "proprietary music," your own horse riding song, will add meaning.

Running away: some countermeasures

Even though you take every precaution, and have dead bolt locks on every room in your house, your venturesome Peter sometimes runs away. You can consider some measures to help find him rapidly, and some to help others identify him and contact you.

Write your phone number on the rim of his shoes with indelible marker.

Write his name, address, and phone on his clothing, or use woven labels if your child can tolerate them.

If he will carry it, get him a cellphone and leave it on (this enables GPS tracking). Recharge it while he is sleeping. Cover it in a waterproof case.

If he will tolerate it, you can try an identity bracelet with contact information.

Train your dog to find him. Some herding dogs will do this without training. Parents of one determined runner report that their black Labrador retriever Riley was a natural runaway tracker, barking as he dashed away after the escapee.

Talk to all the neighbors, and, if they are cooperative and not too busy, the local police. Leave photos and contact information. If possible, organize an informal neighborhood watch so that any adult who sees Peter unaccompanied will collar him and call you immediately.

If you use social media or texting, consider creating a flash mob search party the minute Peter vanishes.

Secondarily, teach Peter to swim as soon as possible. If you can use a pool where they will allow Peter to "fall" in with his clothes on, so that you can drownproof him—i.e. make sure that he can STILL swim if he happens to wind up in the water clothed—so much the better.

When you discover that he is gone, consider where he might have been attracted to, for sensory reasons, or what places he has visited in the past. Do the neighbors have a new trampoline? Is a pool under construction nearby?

If your child loves water, he probably headed to the closest source: check the canal, the lake, the ocean, the bay, the river, the pond, your neighbor's fountain, even the bucket in the back garden, right away.

Be especially vigilant about your exterior door locks in bad weather. Post a sign on your doors so that visiting adults will know why they should keep the doors latched or locked.

Screaming when you turn the car

Your child may have an extremely sensitive inner ear. (If so, he probably has the balance equivalent of perfect pitch, too. He will be able to ride a horse backwards while catching beanbags, and other tricks.) But this sensitivity may be so great that he will scream when you are driving, at the slightest turn of the steering wheel.

Since you seldom drive only in a straight line, this screaming will become a bore. You must do something about it, for the sake of yourself, your child, and any other siblings who may be sitting in the back seat with your Chandler. What you must do is understand the cause. If your Chandler is hypersensitive to sound, he may also be hypersensitive to changes in speed and direction, which are felt in the inner ear. He is not screaming to be an annoyance; he is screaming in panic at the tidal wave of sensations engulfing him. He will not be able to stop because you tell him to; he will not be reassured when you tell him there is no cause for alarm. Why? Because this is a sensory based problem in a neurologically atypical child, with little ability to do any gate-keeping of his own sensations.

In the long term, a specialist may be able to desensitize your Chandler with some auditory training or other intervention. But in the meantime, you need a simple solution. You want to average out the sensory input, adding some calming, rewarding sensations to the deluge.

Try this: Neutralize the panic with a comparable, and simultaneous, happy sensation. We chose a small piece of candy when we worked this out with our son. For six weeks, every time we began to turn the steering wheel, we reached into the back seat simultaneously and gave Ben a piece of candy, not before and not after, but just as the turn was beginning. We did this consistently, without exception and without comment, every trip, for six weeks. For that extended time, as the change in direction, angle, and acceleration to which our Ben seemed to be sensitive was taking place, he was also feeling happy and centered as he sucked on a piece of candy, which, we might add, also exerts a little pressure on the ears.

So you can try neutralizing sensory-induced panic with a simultaneous flood of agreeable sensations.

After those six weeks, we heard no more screaming: Ben was able to accept the cascading sensory information, gain control of himself, and stop screaming. No more candy was needed, nor did he continue to expect it, i.e., the tactic worked.[3] Try it for your Chandler. But if he has a sister, you will have to give her some candy too.

Spinning

Your child with autism may spin around in place, sometimes for several seconds or a minute, without getting dizzy, and evidently without spotting a fixed point visually as ballerinas do. If your Joshua spins, the best bet is that he is giving himself sensory input which he needs. You can try doing it with him, and taking turns to make it interactive, and you can try teaching him dance steps, but the underlying need may persist.

---

3   This is a case that will not respond well to typical parenting options ("Chandler, that's enough!") or ABA techniques; for example, extinguishing screaming by ignoring or penalizing it. A person applying standard ABA methods would not try this sensory averaging tactic because it appears to reward ("reinforce") "bad" behavior. The erroneous ABA expectations would be that, henceforth, candy would always be required for car trips, or even that the child would scream for the rest of his life whenever he wanted candy. Not so. This example shows that ABA approaches for some children simply do not offer the hands-on help parents need, because they are based on a misunderstanding of the dynamics of autism.

You can help him feel spinning forces, if you have a little open space and he is small, by holding him by the wrists, leaning back and spinning yourself, just quickly enough to lift him carefully off the ground as you do. Obviously, don't try this on uneven ground, with wet hands, or if you are unsure of your strength and ability to do this safely.

Pay attention to your Joshua as he spins. If he always spins counter-clockwise, that is the force he craves. You choose that direction too.

Some children's parks have merry-go-rounds. You can give your Samuel a lot of spinning sensation on those if you are willing to push for a while. Consider using his preferred direction.

You can also try taking him to an amusement park or a fair where some of the rides will provide spinning sensations. Don't do THAT if you are not confident he will remain safely seated. The large carousels with wooden animals to ride may be fun but rarely go fast enough to meet your Simon's desire for spinning.

Parents' warning: be aware that some autistic children develop a seizure disorder, and that a seizure may manifest itself in spinning. If your Xavier is running while the seizure starts, he may spin as he loses direction but not momentum. If you see anything odd in your Xavier's spin, catch him.

Spitting

Spitting as a ritual or a sensory-based habit can be tricky to transform. Parents report their children with autism developing complex spitting routines, including one the parents called "the sunburst," which was produced by their well-hydrated son spitting through the gaps in his baby teeth.

The opportunities to make spitting truly interactive may be few, but you can try, in natural contexts such as brushing teeth or using mouthwash, if you care to, because the interactive element will help bring spitting under control. Try brushing your teeth at the same time that your child is brushing his, and then taking turns spitting. This will present some obstacles to your narrating, but give it your best shot. Even better if a sibling can take turns with your spitter, while you narrate.

Tip # 99: Try to transform spitting into blowing.

You can also try to eradicate spitting by transforming it into blowing. To try that, take your little Henry somewhere where he can spit, such as the bathroom sink or drain, and take turns spitting. Then try to introduce a blowing toy, such as bubbles, a whistle, or one of those paper party favors that unfurl. Take a few turns with that, and then return to a spit or two.

You may need to try several different blowing routines or other tongue exercises to take the force out of spitting. You are working against the delightful dramatic effect your Henry will perceive if he spits ON someone outside your home, a drama which he will most likely treasure and try to repeat.

You could also try a substitute mouth activity such as gum chewing that requires some attention but motivates your Henry to keep his mouth closed, and gives him much-needed deep joint pressure at the jaw.

Good luck.

Transitions

Transitions from one place or one activity to another, or from a school schedule to a vacation schedule, may be extremely disconcerting for your child with autism.

You can reduce future transition problems by maintaining as much continuity as possible. If you know that your child will be out of school for several days, ask the teacher to call her and speak to her by phone every day, just to keep alive your child's understanding that school is still part of her experience. If you have photos of the teacher, show your child the photo while the teacher is speaking to her. Try a series of photos in a social story to explain the sequence of events during the holiday.

Although your Eli may be happy to be home from school, he may need to make the transition graphic by going in and out of your door a few times. Let him; this can help him convince himself of the reality of his arrival at home.

Although your young Ben may wish to come inside after playing in the sandbox for a while, he may find the transition itself difficult, even though he wants to make it.

You can help make it easier for your Ben to surmount his transition problems and be able to come inside without losing his self-control. Try some of these options:

- You can make transitions from outdoors to indoors easier by illustrating the most direct way in.

- Depending on your circumstances, you may be able to make your illustration with bright-colored chalk on a walkway, with a path of mulch, with a line of flags, or with a string of pennants, patio lights, or balloons you can tie from the sandbox to the back door, actually connecting the sandbox and the house entrance visibly and physically.

- For a nervous Ben who needs a lot of reassurance, you can try a length of bright-colored rope on the ground, or tied at handrail level if this is safe.

- If you have some tires and boards you use for your obstacle course or for elevation, arrange them so that they connect the sand box and the back door, at least partially.

Tip # 100: For almost any transition from place to place, you can have your child carry some tangible reminder from the first location to the second, some material object meaningful to your child.

If possible, connect that object to the next activity, to establish a link.

Physical reminders of continuity may help your autistic child. If Ben is ready to come inside, have him hold some sand in his hand as he walks up to the house. This carry-over can help reassure him that he can still have fun another time; the sandbox will be there. You can make a game of having him throw his bit of sand, or tuck it neatly into a flower pot, as he approaches the back door.

If your Jeremy is going to kindergarten but has a tough transition to the bus, let him take his teddy bear or another reassuring item providing continuity from home. Later on it can be a photo of the teddy bear, or a miniature teddy bear on a clip. Or photos of his parents and his house may work.

Whenever possible in transitions, transfer your child physically by giving his hand to a person at the new location. "Hello, Auntie Trilby. Here is Ben." "Ben, you go with Auntie Trilby." A physical handover is more likely to succeed.

Tips for longer trips

If you are traveling, provide a photo of the destination if you can. You may be able to find a suitable image on the web. Let your child see it in advance, or at least by the time you are leaving. Take it with you so you can match it to the place when you arrive, adding concrete meaning to the picture. If possible, for older children and those who are already reading, label the photo appropriately, for example, "Auntie

Julie's house," "Grandmother Eleanor's cottage," or "Uncle Indu's office."

Use photos showing what you will do and who you will see when you arrive.

Try using a sequential strip of photos showing each stage of the trip, landmarks along the way, or any place you anticipate stopping for food or a break. A strip showing the return trip might help as well. Many parents use laminated photos with velcro backs.

Downloading the images on the Internet, for example in Google Maps™, you can construct a visual illustration of a trip by showing the street-level views, which are continuous for many streets and roads globally. You could also capture and print snapshots of the major intersections and landmarks on the way, to inform your child with autism fairly accurately what the trip will actually look like.

Another option, often effective, and widely recommended, but time-consuming, is to make the trip in advance with someone recording it on video, perhaps with an iPad®. You can then show this video to your child, if he has the patience to watch the whole thing.

Consider adding meaning by bringing with you some characteristic items; for example, "We are taking your Grandmother some flowers," or, "We are bringing our canvas bags to the market." Try singing songs specific to the destination, or songs that are particularly comforting to your child. A few well-selected toys, such as an airplane for a plane trip, or a toy car steering wheel for trips in the car, can add meaning and a sense of participation. Your child can turn his toy steering wheel as your driver turns, or he can hand-fly his toy plane in a steep climb as your plane taxies down the runway and takes off.

Why this can work:

It maximizes the amount of information you make available to all senses, to increase clarity and comprehension and to reduce anxiety about the unknown. Touch, sound, taste, smell, and sight may all be informative and calming to your child. To the extent that your Nathan participates in the trip and acts out its meaning, his comprehension increases and his anxiety decreases.

With practice, in the long term your child may be able to generalize trip taking, and then will rely less on these aids.

If the toys become ballistic missiles, we don't have to tell you to confiscate them.

About travel by car in general: if you have child safety locks preventing your child from opening the door on her own, use them. Do not forget the lock on the back hatch, if your car has one.

Waiting, or not being able to

Concretizing the meaning of some time intervals may help. External cues about time, which give intervals of time a physical meaning, may help your Poppy wait more calmly. You can try clock faces with a red sector that gradually disappears as the time elapses, or perhaps a set of little transparent hourglass timers that run out of sand in one, two, three, five, and ten minutes. Give these intervals real, immediate meaning. For example, set the clock timer so that the batch of cookies is done when the time is up and the red sector has completely disappeared. You can tell your Poppy, "The cookies will be ready in five minutes." Have her playing nearby, but keeping an eye on the red sector clock. The instant the red sector vanishes, jump up and get the cookies.

Similarly, have in mind a set of events that will take place at one, two, three, five, and ten minutes, to correspond to the moment the sand runs out in each hourglass.

Your child may already have a clear comprehension of how long his speech therapy sessions are, or how long a class lasts. You can try to connect this awareness with a clock, and the idea of an hour.

At the most fundamental level, giving your child with autism many opportunities to sequence photos of events and processes she knows may also help establish the ability to wait.

Some distractions are a good idea also. If your Poppy can listen to music on her iPod® while she waits, or look at a book, or play with a fidget toy, so much the better.

Walking on tiptoes

Tip # 101: For the child who walks on tiptoes often, offer edge experiences and enrich all his sensations.

Even a small amount of elevation may increase your sensory-hungry Mason's awareness of his body, so he may like to walk on tiptoes to feel this increased height, and to increase his sense of his own weight.

You may find that your Mason will walk flat-footed on an elevated surface such as a picnic bench or a low stone wall.

He may be one of the ASD children who crave the heightened sensations of edge experiences, by which we mean both the experience of reinforcing where your body ends, and the thrill of positioning yourself near edges, where you will be aware of heights. You can try offering these experiences to Mason whenever possible.

Again consider talking with your physician about whether some natural source vitamin A, such as that in cod liver oil, might help Mason experience his body more fully.

You can easily offer several kinds of edge experiences which increase your child's body awareness:

- Climbing,[4] for example on outdoor play equipment, on a rock wall in a gym, in a tree, on a pile of tires, or on several bales of hay.

- Swinging forcefully, especially in a very long arc, as on a rope swing from a tall tree out over a lawn that drops away, or, on shorter swings, swinging so powerfully that Mason is almost horizontal.[5]

- For a child who knows how to swim, swinging out over a swimming area and dropping in would be ideal.

- Squeezing or applying firm consistent pressure to large areas of the body, via a squeeze machine, a firm hug, a "Mason sandwich" made up of Mason between two gym pads, with a friend lying on top like garnish; crawling through a constricted toy fabric tunnel.

- Walking on elevated surfaces, such as a garden wall, possibly holding your hand; walking with one foot on the curb and the other in the gutter; balancing on a narrow board, balance beam, plank, or fence rail on the ground or only a few inches above it.

---

4   An intensely sensory-hungry ASD child like your Mason may climb up on your furniture and try to walk on the backs. This tells you to provide an enriched sensory diet for him, and to consider working with him while he is elevated.

5   This experience is fruitful enough for some nonverbal ASD children that they may be able to make several sounds or say a word while swinging. A skilled speech therapist might work with your child before, during, or after swinging.

Trouble-shooting when nothing works

Is your Cody making you crazy with some new trick you really want to discourage but do not even understand? Dr. Miller would suggest some set questions to try to analyze the problem.

Example:

Suppose your Cody has always loved water, and used to play outdoors in the water from the hose with delight. You have seen him before scooping water out of the dog dish and flipping it into the air. But now he is also drinking out of the dog dish, and you naturally find this revolting.

Dr. Miller would ask: What does this new development mean?

To help you form some idea of its meaning, Dr. Miller would ask some supporting questions about Cody sharing the dog's water:

When Cody drinks out of the dog dish, is he looking at you or at anyone else?

If so, he is probably trying to communicate something, to the person he is looking at. Could he be waiting for, and hoping to cause, a dramatic emotional reaction?

Is he communicating with you about crossing the boundaries of acceptable behavior, or could he be communicating with you about imitating the dog?

Or both?

If you think his main purpose is to stimulate a strong emotional response from you, why not try a chasing game somewhere else ("I'm going to GET you!")? That will probably derail the dog dish drinking bouts.

If chasing does not seem dramatic enough to Cody, try a game involving water, such as tossing water balloons, or squirting each other with water toys reciprocally.

On the other hand, if you think your Cody is actually playing a game with himself in which he is imitating your dog drinking, this is GREAT and is a step toward symbolic reasoning. You could try to expand the dog drinking imitation by supplying a large toy dog or a large cardboard cutout dog which Cody could pretend to help to drink. This too might substitute for Cody's desire to drink your dog's water, and actually is symbolic play. (Why are we so excited about symbolic play? Because it stimulates higher order reasoning and speech.)

If you think both features are at work—Cody wants more attention from you and is also imitating your dog—it might be time for feeding and watering the dog to be Cody's job, if it isn't already. Help him get started. You may need to supervise for a while.

How to take advantage of playtime for therapeutic purposes: install cheap sensory equipment for your back garden, yard, or any suitable open space

If your child craves height, motion, edge experiences, and intense sensations of many kinds, you can make available outside opportunities to meet those needs. A park nearby may be perfect. If not, you can do it yourself:

For elevation

For children who love heights, create a safe way to elevate your kid by putting two stable picnic table benches together. If materials and money allow, build a treehouse, acquire a swing set with an elevated fort, or even just a few tires that can be stacked. It's even better if they are different sizes. Old tree stumps or sections of logs can work as well. Bales of straw to stack are excellent.

If you have room and the materials are available, you can use old tires and planks to make elevated structures for the kids to walk and play on. If you connect the swings to the sandbox using an elevated walkway, all the play equipment will get more use.

If your Aubrey would benefit from having her outdoor play spots connected so that her transitions between them are easier, and tires and planks are not an option, you can use powdered chalk on the ground, or strings of small pennants tied from the back door to the swings, a tree, a hammock, or other attractions.

For motion and speed

For children who need intense input, try a swing that can move through a very wide arc over land that drops away or changes elevation.

Also consider a smaller swing that can have a spring in the chain or rope somewhere, to vary the sensation by bouncing while swinging.

For texture

Consider a sand pit or a sandbox with a cover, or fill an old tire with clean washed play sand, pea gravel, aquarium stones, bark chips, or whatever heavily textured materials are available. We know a teacher[6] who, one fall when the oak trees exceeded themselves, gathered a crate full of acorns for her favorite charge to play with.

---

6   Yes, Michelle Hanrahan Heckman, this means you!

For water play

Ideally, flowing water in creeks and rivers, or surging water in the sea, would be a delight for your sensory-seeking child. If these sources are not available or are not clean, consider other ways to make water play accessible.

A bucket, a shallow baby pool, an old dish pan, a shallow livestock watering container, or a pan for mixing concrete all work well to hold water for splashing. What about a pond liner? Empty periodically to avoid mosquitos, unexpected frogs, etc.

Also consider sprinklers; a hose with or without an adjustable nozzle, or an old hose with holes in it; a baby pool with a central spot to thread a hose through, to create a cheap fountain.

For visual interest

Consider cloth flags, pinwheels, pennants, banners, feather flags, and ribbons to catch the breezes.

For sound

Wind chimes, falling water, or rustling bead curtains.

An obstacle course in the back yard is a fun opportunity to develop coordination and speed. Consider laying out a pattern of old tires, low barriers to jump over, a small sandpit to jump into, vertical poles or flags to run around as on a ski slope, etc. If you supervise or participate, you have an ideal opportunity to teach signs such as up, down, in, out, over, under, through.

And for meeting almost every sensory need, if you live in or near an agricultural area, a hayride in the fall may be your child's nirvana.

At the beach or the lake with your child who needs structure

Your sensory-hungry Ryan may be thrilled with the sand and the pull of the waves at the beach, but he may be able to enjoy the beach more with a little definition of space. You might, too, if he is able to stay with you happily without continually running away. If a beach umbrella and chairs do not give enough structure to allow your Ryan to settle in, consider some other ways to create a defined space he can recognize at the shore, on the lake, or at a campsite:

- Pitch a pop-up tent or a larger tent; dig a deep spot to sit in, if the tent is floorless. Weight the tent with sand. Know where the high tide line is.

- Use a beach windscreen or two to make a corral.

- Spread rice straw mats or beach towels on the sand, to define a sitting area or a walkway; or hang them from strings.

- Dig a trench in the sand around your little settlement.

- Bring a small inflatable pool; blow it up and fill it with sand or seawater as desired. It serves as a sandbox, or a water play spot, or, when dry, a playpen for smaller kids.

- Set up four beach chairs in a square, perhaps with an umbrella over them.

- If possible, bring a cooler; pack your refreshments in ice cubes or crushed ice you can give Ryan to play with or eat.

Another household problem
parents tell us about: laundry

Everyone with a family and without a personal laundry service has laundry problems. But you, with your child with autism, have a laundry calamity.

Why, you may ask, will the adults never have clean clothes themselves?

Well, your Reginald will like to play in the sand/mud/water, and he will require a change of clothing every time he comes into the house; unless, of course, you wisely hose him down on the back porch, or are living in a beach house where you can throw him in the outdoor shower. Or you can train him to change his clothes just inside the back door, and re-use the dirty ones, perhaps gaily festooning the porch railing or the deck with them.

When one mother tried that recycling trick, her Aaron's shirt sleeves filled up with yellowjackets, which she found as they were stinging Aaron's elbows and flying out of the shirtsleeves in an unattractive frame of mind.

(Note: Yellowjackets can find zippers that are not completely closed.)

Why else might you never have clean clothes?

Well, your Jackson will HATE the mere THOUGHT of dirt and come weeping and gasping for a new shirt every time a mote of dust touches him. Or even a photon, on a bad day. Esmeralda will prefer her pink party dress (or her white tutu, or the Halloween costume in which she was a green peapod) for every occasion and to all other clothing on earth. She may wear it out in the snow, to funerals, etc., and be disconsolate and unbearable if it isn't always freshly laundered and ready to be enjoyed.

And then, your Brandon is a light sleeper and will leap out of bed the moment he hears either the washer or the dryer. Side payment: if you put the baby on the dryer in her carrier, the vibration may lull her to sleep.

Do you really think *YOUR* clothes are getting washed, when you are keeping up with THAT?

Solution: There is no solution. But you could try putting one item of your clothing in every load of wash you do.

Intermezzo

The specific gravity of seersucker: a series of unforeseen events

Your child is old enough to take a bath unsupervised. He has popped out of the bathtub and disappeared down the hall in a shower of droplets and soap bubbles, giggling. You dash to the bathroom to gather the towels.

A "no textiles" day has apparently been declared in your bathroom: all the towels, washcloths, and the bathmat are balled up on the floor, soggy.

Your curtains are not hanging in the window. They are not on the floor. They are not in the laundry. They are not in the trash.

The curtains are gone.

The curtain rod has been replaced on its hooks, rocking.

The toilet is gurgling quietly.

Your curtains have been buried at sea.

10

CONCLUSION

Key points:

Children with autism are often extremely bright. But you must address their multiple intensive needs so that their light can shine in the world.

Your goal is twofold: not only do you want to help your Evan develop all his capacities as rapidly as possible; you also want to transform your Evan's unacceptable and annoying behavior into more appropriate conduct and more fulfilling engagement with the world. He may need to pick up a whole constellation of routines that he might have missed, which children typically pick up as they grow, such as body control to allow hopping, skipping, riding a scooter or a bike, and routine use of objects including tools.

He also needs to learn to communicate as effectively as he can as soon as possible. You can help him.

About communication

Remember that your Ruby needs motivation to learn new signs. She is more likely to want to learn dramatic action words like "run" and "jump" than protocol-conscious words and phrases such as "excuse me," "thank you," and "good morning," which may mean little to her.

Dyspraxia or apraxia combined with autism may mean that your Clayton needs frequent reinforcement with his signing, may tolerate and need hand-over-hand assistance or parallel assistance with his signing from time to time. Also, like a typical language user, he needs to keep his words and signs in frequent use so that they do not get rusty.

Don't get discouraged if Clayton does not regain speech right away; he can (re-) learn to talk at any age, like anyone else needing rehabilitation. But be sure he gets a speech therapist with a record of success with apraxic children. If your therapist tells you rehabilitation is impossible, get a new therapist.

Remember to narrate often with your Clayton, and sign while you do so. When you speak to him, remember that he may be able to listen better if he has something in his hands.

Remember that it may be easier for your children with autism to finish an interrupted sentence than it is for them to answer questions, whether they are signing, speaking, using PECS, an assistive communication device, or some combination of communication modes.

A few memorable relating rules for every interaction

Whenever you play with your Mila, ask yourself:

Am I starting off with some exciting, repetitive, big body activity such as pushing, pulling, lifting, carrying, dropping, jumping, running, or stomping? For a smaller child, am I thinking about tossing her in the air over a soft landing sofa, or something equally fun and dramatic? This will help develop her body awareness and focus.

Am I elevating Mila when it would be helpful and safe to do so?

When I talk to my Mila, do I comment on something distinctive about her each time?

Am I trying to work with her at her eye level?

Am I narrating for Mila, with signs and spoken words, describing what she is doing while she is doing it, to make her vocabulary grow?

Can I learn to be specific instead of constantly relying on, "Good job!" which may mean about as much to my Mila as it does to my dachshund? "Mila tied her shoe, hurray!" is much more specific than, "Good job, Mila!" even if she hears my approval in each exclamation.

Do I make it my business to learn all the signs I need to make word meanings more vivid and interesting to my Mila?[1] Do I sign with her all the time?

When I sing for my Mila, am I choosing songs for meaning and relevance to her experience, or am I stuck with "Eentsy, Weensy Spider"? Do I work to concretize each song I sing for my child?[2]

Do I seize any opportunities Mila shows me for developing some relevant concepts or functions? If she disappears under my sheets, do I know how to exploit that by, for example, exclaiming in mock dismay, "Oh no! My Mila is GONE! Where can she BE? Is she HERE?" (pat pat).

If Mila does not know how to draw, or has been compelled at school to do something pointless like endlessly filling in pre-drawn shapes, do I think of ways to get her started scribbling and enjoying it, perhaps coloring heavily on a page with a leaf underneath to make the leaf appear, or tracing around real objects of interest, or circling some bright stickers of birds, cars, and people, or using other tricks to make it fun to represent things?

---

1   If you cannot take a signing course, many reliable books and computer programs can help, such as, in the US, *Signing Exact English*, Gerilee Gustason and Esther Zawolkow (1993). Unfortunately there is no global standard for signed English; systems vary by country and region.

2   One parent tells us she was so tired when her child was small that often all she could remember to sing for him when he needed a lullaby was "Old Stewball was a Racehorse."

When we are traveling, do I remember to point out landmarks and symbols she may recognize?

When we are celebrating our holidays, do I think of ways to make them meaningful for Mila?

You have arrived at the end of the Miller field manual for parents of children with autism. We offer you three final bonus tips as a reward.

Two parent tips:

1. When you get the autism diagnosis, find an education and special needs lawyer right away. You will need one.[3]

2. For the next 20 years, think twice before you go to the potty.

And the last and best tip, in the immortal words of Dr. Arnold Miller:

"Don't give autism too much respect. Get in its face."

---

3   This footnote is courtesy of Dr. Bruce Edward Auerbach, and he should know.

Finale—Jellyfish in your hat

It is a sunny day at the beach. Your precious child is lying on his belly in the shallow seawater, remembering surfing. He is floating a few inches above the rippled sand, carried back and forth by the current.

You spot, about three feet away, a small red jellyfish, also carried by the current. Each wave rocks him and his little stingy tentacles closer to your child's tender calves.

What to do? You can't leave the child to go get a bucket; he might spring up and run into the sea; he might get caught in the undertow. But he won't get up to escape; he is in sensory heaven. And you can't let a jellyfish sting him.

Hissing, the waves rush up the scorching beach; undulating, the jellyfish swoops through the water, and you, before you know it, scoop him up in your baseball cap.

C'est la vie.

AFTERWORD FROM ETHAN B. MILLER

In writing the book *101 Tips for Parents of Children with Autism*, on the Miller Method®, Theresa C. Smith has done a great service for me personally, for my family, and to the memory of Dr. Arnold Miller and Eileen Eller-Miller. This much-needed book was one of the projects my father believed in strongly, and had hoped to see completed. Sadly, it was not to be. That Theresa would deliver on this project is testimony to her belief in the Miller Method®, and it is because of this and the many contributions she and her husband, Dr. Bruce Auerbach, have made, that they are on the Honor Roll of the LCDC in Newton, Massachusetts.

That Theresa could incorporate the many theoretical fine points described in my father's first book, *From Ritual to Repertoire* (1989), and the practical applications of his second book, *The Miller Method®* (2007), into her and Bruce's own journey with their son, Ben, shows their understanding of the subject matter. That she could make their own story accessible to others, in effect telling other parents that they are not alone, and that help is at hand, demonstrates the kind of people they are.

From this book, a parent will discover that the Miller Method® works. It is not the answer to every disorder for every child, but it offers a natural, intuitive approach to teaching these children, allowing the skillful practitioner to reach into their world and draw them out. You will find many helpful techniques in this book, applied in real life situations (at times hilarious and at other times heartbreaking), as well as a rational explanation of why they are used.

In my mind, what would have made my father most satisfied, is that Theresa never leaves out the theoretical underpinnings he developed, derived from his teacher Dr. Heinz Werner and others. At the heart of the Miller Method® is adaptability, but never without a grounding in psychological theory. Dad never deviated from scientific methodology in developing his theory or applying technique. These days, the LCDC is venturing more deeply into research, which will no doubt provide more confirmation for the method. Increasing the evidence base for the Miller Method® and making more people aware of it would have been Dr. Miller's ultimate satisfaction. It is with great thanks to Theresa and to Bruce that I write this afterword.

Ethan B. Miller
Director of Operations, LCDC
Newton, Massachusetts
USA
June 25, 2013

APPENDIX 1

How You Can Toilet Train your Spectrum Child with Help from Your Doctor[1]

Based on the Work of the eminent Dr. Mary N. Megson[2]

If your beloved child with autism is oblivious to toilet training, an underlying biological deficit may be the problem. Many children with autism cannot be toilet-trained, not because they don't want to or because they are inattentive, but because they cannot feel the impulses telling them when they need to go to the bathroom. Consult your doctor about this possibility.

A solution, if the obstacle is sensation-based, and possibly vitamin A-related, is to enhance these sensations for your children, and accustom them to toilet training, with a change in diet, some supplements, and a medicine your physician can prescribe.

This appendix summarizes our experience following the advice of Dr. Mary N. Megson, Richmond, VA. Dr. Megson is a board-certified pediatrician, Fellowship-trained in child development, and a member of the American Academy of Pediatrics. She has practiced pediatrics for more than 30 years, seeing children with developmental disabilities, which include learning disabilities, attention deficit hyperactivity disorder, cerebral palsy, mental retardation, and autism.

---

1 And a nutritionist wouldn't hurt, either.
2 Dr. Megson's website and contact information can be found at www.megson.com.

1) First, eliminate your child's exposure to vitamin A palmitate. This is a five-branched form of vitamin A which is shelf-stable for long periods. It is routinely added to baby formula, children's cereals, many baked goods, and other foods, drinks, snacks, some candy, and cosmetics, in the USA and elsewhere. In the USA it is present in all reduced fat milk; consequently, it may be present in any foods made with reduced fat milk, even if the label does not list it. It is also added to margarine.

If your child attends daycare or school, where they may be given food or drinks, try to get the staff to cooperate with your plan to prevent your child from being exposed to vitamin A palmitate. If necessary, pack and send separate drinks, snacks, and lunches for your child, because probably the margarine avoidance by itself means that your child cannot eat in the school cafeteria. Be sure your child avoids all such foods while you are toilet-training.[3]

Getting all vitamin A palmitate out of your child's diet means making sure that his food, drinks, snacks, condiments, frozen treats, or even candy do not contain it.[4] Check the labels to see that vitamin A palmitate is not present in any supplements or medicines your child uses, such as fluoride drops,[5] gummy vitamins, or multivitamins.

Watch for unexpected exposures to vitamin A palmitate in lotions, shampoos, and sunscreens. Unfortunately, vitamin A palmitate is widely dispersed in toiletries and in the food

---

3   Later it may not be so important if you are providing a good source of the cis-form of vitamin A, which is found in cod liver oil.

4   Ingredients have become difficult to verify in the US because of recent changes in the labeling law allowing manufacturers to call small amounts of some ingredients, such as saturated fats, zero. However, vitamin A palmitate seems to be seen as "enriching," so may be likely to be listed.

5   Think twice before using fluoride, as it disrupts G series proteins in some cases.

supply. Consider giving your child whole milk if they are a milk drinker.

2) Give cod liver oil. Unless he is allergic, start giving your child with autism at least ½ a teaspoon of refrigerated cod liver oil every day, or the equivalent in capsules. A larger child at around 100 lbs might use a whole teaspoon. You can determine the correct amount and source for your child in consultation with your physician or a nutritionist.[6] If you use liquid cod liver oil, do not forget to store it in the refrigerator.

Be certain that your cod liver oil is certified to be free of heavy metals. Keep giving it every day. In three months, the cis form of vitamin A in cod liver oil will have primed your child's neurological pump, to get your child's receptors ready to feel toilet training sensations. Other improvements may happen while you are waiting.

3) Add beta carotene. Since you are emphasizing vitamin A, try adding natural, vitamin A-rich foods to your child's diet if he is not already enjoying sweet potatoes, squash, pumpkin, apricots, etc. In the USA, a convenient way to succeed easily in increasing your child's intake of natural vitamin A as beta carotene is to offer him V8 Splash®, V8 V-Fusion®, and similar drinks which contain liquefied carrots. Or make them yourself. Do not worry about overdosing. No amount of beta carotene is toxic.

4) Try bethanecol. Now consult your doctor about the appropriateness of using bethanecol, also called urecholine, to stimulate your child to feel potty training nerve impulses. Your doctors can calculate the dose and frequency for your child and prescribe it if they think it is indicated. Your child may be sensitive to bethanecol, so some doctors will suggest

---

6   You can find further dosing instructions at this website: http://kirkmanlabs.com/ProductKirkman/218/1/Product%20Details.

you build up gradually to an effective dose. They may suggest, for example, that you begin using 2.5 mg capsules, one twice a day. Every three to five days, you might add another capsule two times a day, until you reach the amount your doctor has recommended.

5) Keep on explaining. While you are laying the biochemical foundation for toilet training for your child, keep giving many opportunities and examples about toileting, using whatever works best with your child, such as photos, pictures, a video, an example from an appropriate adult, or sibling, etc. You may want to post visual directions in the bathroom for your child to consult. If you use a toilet seat inset so your child cannot fall in, and you need the little deflector, consider using one that does not have what looks like the surface of a ginger grater on the inside. Your child is not going to like the look of that.

Steady on with this. Do not lose heart. One day your child may just run in from outside and spontaneously use the potty, as our Ben did, because now he can feel it. This breakthrough can take any amount of time from a few weeks to a few months, but typically at least 30 days. Be patient and treat misses with calm and dignity.

Our Ben gained control over pooping promptly but complete control over peeing took him about three months. We still needed waterproof sheets for a time.

When you have achieved the results you want, and your child is no longer the oldest kid on the playground still in pull-ups, you must judge when to stop using bethanecol, or cut back, because it can overstimulate your child. Consult your physician in all aspects of this project.

Parent's note: For our Ben this process was permanent and prompt. If your child's problem is vitamin A-related insensitivity, your experience should be similar.

APPENDIX 2
If You Want to Know More

I. Contacts

Language and Cognitive Development Center
Ethan B. Miller, Director of Operations
154 Wells Avenue, Suite 5
Newton, MA 02459
USA
Tel: (800) 218 LCDC (5232)
(617) 965 0045
Fax: (617) 965 0289
Email: emiller115@gmail.com

II. Websites on the Miller Method® and Miller Method® materials

www.millermethod.org—This is the central website for the Miller Method®. It features news and instruction about upcoming training workshops, as well as information and publications concerning the Miller Method® and links to other Miller Method® sites.

www.cognitivedesigns.com—This website offers books and materials on the Miller Method®, including the Sign and Spoken language program, and the SARP.

http://millermethodcommunity.ning.com—The Community website provides discussion forums, a blog, and information about applying the Miller Method®. Membership is free.

www.rebeccasperbermft.com/millerMethod.htm—This is the website for the Los Angeles Miller Method® Resource Center, directed by Rebecca Sperber, M.S., M.F.T.

III. Miller Method®-affiliated schools

Crossroads School is the largest Miller Method® school in the USA.

Crossroads School
Michael J. Kowalski, Principal
45 Cardinal Drive
Westfield, NJ 07090
USA
Tel: (908) 232 6655
Email: mkowalski@ucesc.org
http://ucesc.org/ucesc/Schools & Services/Crossroads School

These schools employ a variety of approaches, including the Miller Method®.

A Starting Place
Patricia Dorsey, Principal
664 Orangeburg Rd.
Pearl River, NY 10965
USA
Tel: (845) 7353 066
Email: astartingplace@gmail.com

Alia for Early Intervention
Rania Al Khalifa, Director
Mailing address:
Post Office Box 37304
Kingdom of Bahrain
Tel: +973 17 730960
Fax: +970 17 737227
Email: autism@batelco.com.bh
http://www.childbehavior.org
School located at:
Building 5
Road 1115
Block 611
Sitra,
Kingdom of Bahrain

Bahrain Society for Children with Behavioral and Communication Difficulties
Associated with the Alia for Early Intervention school
www.childbehavior.org/home.html

Alokdhara School
Mrs. Krishna Roy, Principal
1/2 D Bosepukur Road, Prantik Pally
Kolkata 700 042
India
Tel: +91 33 64508205
Email: query@aiokdhara-inclusion.org
http://alokdhara-inclusion.org

IV. Selected sources of information on autism

ASPEN

9 Aspen Circle
Edison, NJ 08820
USA
Tel: (732)3210 880
www.aspennj.org

Asperger's Syndrome Education Network: A national nonprofit organization headquartered in New Jersey that provides education and support to families and individuals affected by Asperger's syndrome, PDD-NOS, high-functioning autism, and related disorders.

Autism-PDD Resources Network

Advocates of inclusion
Autism-PDD.NET
14271 Jeffrey #3
Irvine, CA 92620
USA
www.autism-pdd.net

Autism Society of America

7910 Woodmont Ave., Suite 650
Bethesda, MD 20814–3 015
USA
1 800 3 AUTISM
Tel: (301) 6570 881
Email: veronica.m.zysk@gtees.sprint.com
www.autism-society.org

Autism Speaks

2 Park Avenue, 11th Floor
New York, NY 10016
USA
Tel: (212) 2528 584
Email: familyservices@autismspeaks.org
www.autismspeaks.org

Parents' advocacy group. Our goal is to change the future for all who struggle with ASD. We are dedicated to funding global biomedical research into the causes, prevention, treatments, and cure of autism; to raising public awareness about autism and its effects on individuals, families, and society; and to bringing hope to all who deal with the hardships of this disorder. We are committed to raising the funds necessary to support these goals.

Center for the Study of Autism

The Autism Research Institute of Bernard Rimland, Ph.D.
4182 Adams Avenue
San Diego, CA 92116
Tel: (866) 366 3361
Email: denise@autism.com
www.autism.com

The Interdisciplinary Council on Developmental and Learning Disorders
4938 Hampden Lane Suite 800
Bethesda, Maryland 20814
Tel: (301) 656 2667
Email: info@icdl.com
www.icdl.com

National Autism Center

41 Pacella Park Drive
Randolph, Massachusetts 02368
USA
Tel: (877) 3133833
Email: info@nationalautismcenter.org
www.nationalautismcenter.org

The National Autism Center is a new nonprofit organization dedicated to supporting effective, evidence-based treatment approaches and providing direction to families, practitioners, organizations, policy-makers, and funders. The Center is bringing nationally renowned experts together to establish national treatment standards, model best practices, and conduct applied research, serving as a vital source of information, training, and services.

OASIS

Contacts: Barbara Kirby and Patricia Romanowski Bashe
Mailing address:
P.O. Box 524
Crown Point, IN 46308
Physical address:
950 S. Court St.
Crown Point, IN 46307
Tel: (219) 662 1311
Email: info@asperbersyndrome.com
www.aspergersyndrome.org

Online Asperger Syndrome Information and Support

A national online support group and resource for parents, professionals, and individuals with Asperger Syndrome. Includes online support boards and chatrooms, as well as publications, resources, and other comprehensive information.

GLOSSARY OF SELECTED MILLER TERMS

Elevated Square: Observation shows that many children with ASD improve focus when they are elevated. They may read more proficiently in a treehouse, for example. Wanting an elevated surface for working with children with autism, Dr. Miller developed an Elevated Square structure which is about two and a half feet off the ground, and in some sets of plans measures about 5 × 8 feet, actually a rectangle. See the description and photo in *The Miller Method*® (2007, pp. 90–3), as well as many examples of ways the square catches children with autism and helps them order their actions.

Engagement is active involvement. If your child orients toward a ball with a flashing light in it, and then picks it up and examines it closely, your child is engaged with the ball.

Executive function refers to your child's ability to scan her environment and make choices about which routines she would like to undertake or combine in new ways.

Mutual face-touching: When your Erin repeatedly shows you difficulty with eye contact and poor awareness of other people, or when you are helping her restore equilibrium after a loss of control, you can help her with mutual face-touching. (Also remember that eye contact problems may be caused by poor rod function within the eye, which can clear up with vitamin A from cod liver oil; consult your physician.) Take both of your child's hands in yours and begin hand-over-hand to have her alternately stroke your cheek, while you say, "Mom," or, "Papa," or, "Aunt Trilby," as the case may be, and then her cheek, saying her name. Do this slowly, quietly, and rhythmically, several times, and then abruptly stop, and blow on her hand or nibble on her fingers. The dramatic contrast between quiet, gentle rhythm and the abrupt burst of air on her hand frequently will help your Erin look intently directly at you—to see what is coming next!

Narration is used in Miller Method® programs to help children connect what they hear with what they are doing. Narration is vital for developing receptive and expressive language, as well as enhancing awareness and enjoyment of the self. As a parent, you narrate like a sports announcer, play by play, what your child is doing as she is doing it. "Amalia is riding her bike! She is going by really fast! Now she is waving with her left hand!" Vocal color will enhance your child's understanding.

Orienting is the tendency of your child to turn toward the most salient source of stimulus available. Often, we want this salient source to be you! Become salient by whispering, for example.

Pacing is critical for success with children who find it difficult to get involved with and carry out routines. Often you may need to carry your child with autism quite briskly through an activity or a routine so that he has less chance to lose his grip on what he has just done. Dramatic changes in the course of the routine help, such as walking quickly upstairs and slipping quickly down a slide. Be alert for the need to speed up or slow down to help your child remain connected to his work or play.

PLOP stands for person, location, object, and position. It is an acronym for reminding parents and family members that their child with autism needs to develop all these types of expansions of routines—with different people, in different locations, using different objects, and from different positions—to be sure that she has generalized her knowledge about a particular system or routine.

Restabilizing, previously mentioned as a strategy to guide behavior, can also be helpful to restore your child's contact with you if she seems to be drifting away. You need to repeatedly and unexpectedly pluck at her shirt or her sweater from front to back, and from side to side, tugging gently on her clothing so that you pull your child slightly off-balance. In restoring her balance, your Dale becomes more aware of her own body and is therefore better able to relate to you. Restabilizing for smaller children often works best when your child is elevated, by standing on a chair or bench that brings her up to your eye level. If your child is averse to eye contact for no known medical reason, you can often encourage her to look at you by combining restabilizing with mutual face-touching.

Spontaneous expansions occur when your child deviates from the original, or "prescribed" or conventional, way of doing things. Going down the slide on his back, instead of sitting down, might be an expansion for your Jeremy. Spontaneous expansions are significant precursors of executive function.

System or action system is a repetitive series of actions centered on an event or an object, which your child can carry out unassisted. In this book we have referred to systems as routines. Examples of routines: repeatedly picking up stones and dropping them into a bucket of water; running several cycles in a specified circle.

Zone of intention is the space within which a child on the autism spectrum can most effectively take in new information. Often this space may be no more than 12–18 inches from the child's body, especially soon after onset. Parents need to be aware of their own child's working zone of intention and to systematically expand it so that he can take in information further and further away from his body.

SHORT SELECTED BIBLIOGRAPHY

I. Background

Baio, J. (2012) "Prevalence of autism spectrum disorders—autism and developmental disabilities monitoring network, 14 sites, United States, 2008 surveillance summaries." *Morbidity and Mortality Weekly Report 61*, 1–19.

Bettelheim, B. (1950) *Love is Not Enough: The Treatment of Emotionally Disturbed Children.* New York and Glencoe, IL: Free Press.

Bogdashina, O. (2004) *Sensory Perceptual Issues in Autism and Asperger Syndrome: Different Sensory Experiences—Different Perceptual Worlds.* London: Jessica Kingsley Publishers.

Gustason, G. and Zawolkow, E. (1993) *Signing Exact English.* Los Alamitos, CA: Modern Signs Press.

Hallmayer, J., Cleveland, S., Torres, A., Phillips, J., *et al.* (2011) "Genetic heritability and shared environmental factors among twin pairs with autism." *Archives of General Psychiatry 68*, 11, 1095–1102.

Kanner, L. (1943) "Autistic disturbances of affective contact." *Nervous Child 2*, 217–50.

Kanner, L. (1971) "Follow-up study of 11 autistic children originally reported in 1943." *Journal of Autism and Childhood Schizophrenia 1*, 119–149.

Lovaas, O.I. (1987) "Behavioral treatment and normal educational and intellectual functioning in young autistic children." *Journal of Consulting and Clinical Psychology 55*, 3–9.

Megson, M.N. (2000) "Autism: present challenges, future needs—why the increased rates?" Hearing before the Committee on Government Reform, House of Representatives, One Hundred Sixth Congress, second session, April 6, 2000. US Government Printing Office (2001).

Megson, M.N. (2000) "Is autism a G-alpha protein defect reversible with natural vitamin A?" *Journal of Medical Hypotheses 54*, 6, 979–983.

Rutter, M. (2005) "Incidence of autism spectrum disorders: changes over time and their meaning." *Acta Paediatrica: Nurturing the Child 94*, 1, 2–15.

Skinner, B.F. (1951) "How to Teach Animals." *Scientific American 185*, 26–29.

Smith, T. and Eikeseth, S. (2011) "O. Ivar Lovaas: pioneer of applied behavior analysis and intervention for children with autism." *Journal of Autism and Developmental Disorders 41*, 3, 375–8.

II. Additional information on the Miller Method®

Cook, C.E. (1998) "The Miller Method: a case study illustrating use of the approach with children with autism in an interdisciplinary setting." *Journal of Developmental and Learning Disorders 2*, 2, 231–264.

Cook, C.E. (2001) "The Miller Method: An Early Intervention Program to Help Young Children with Autism Make Meaning in Their Lives." In L.J. Rogers and B.B. Swadener (eds) *Semiotics and Dis/ability: Interrogating Categories of Difference*. Albany, New York: State University of New York Press.

Mastrangelo, S. (2009) "Play and the child with autism spectrum disorder: from possibilities to practice." *International Journal of Play Therapy 18*, 1, 13–30.

Miller, A. (1991) "Cognitive-Developmental Systems Theory in Pervasive Developmental Disorders." In J. Beitchman and M. Konstantareas (eds) *Psychiatric Clinics of North America Volume 14: Pervasive Developmental Disorders*. Philadelphia, PA: W.B. Saunders Press.

Miller, A. with Chrétien, K. (2007) *The Miller Method: Developing the Capacities of Children on the Autism Spectrum*. London: Jessica Kingsley Publishers.

Miller, A. and Eller-Miller, E. (1989) *From Ritual to Repertoire: A Cognitive-Developmental Systems Approach with Disordered Children*. New York: Wiley and Sons.

Miller, A. and Eller-Miller, E. (2000) "The Miller Method: A Cognitive-Developmental Systems Approach for Children with Body Organization, Social and Communication Issues." In S. Greenspan and S. Wieder (eds) *ICDL Clinical Practices Guidelines: Revising the Standards of Practice for Infants, Toddlers and Children with Developmental Challenges*. Bethesda, MD: ICDL.

Miller, A. and Hilliard, C. (2007) "A unique approach to the development of reading skills." *Autism Spectrum Quarterly 7*, 65. Available at www.asquarterly.com/issues/7/articles/65.

Miller, A. and Miller, E. E. (1968) "Symbol accentuation: the perceptual transfer of meaning from spoken to written words." *The American Journal of Mental Deficiency 73*, 200–8.

Miller, A. and Miller, E. E. (1973) "Cognitive-developmental training with elevated boards and sign language." *Journal of Autism and Childhood Schizophrenia 3*, 65–85.

III. Evidence-based research on the Miller Method® and related natural approaches

Delprato, D.J. (2001) "Comparisons of discrete-trial and normalized behavioral language intervention for young children with autism." *Journal of Autism and Developmental Disorders 31*, 3, 315–25.

Sheehy, K. (2005) "Morphing images: a potential tool for teaching word recognition to children with severe learning difficulties." *British Journal of Educational Technology 36*, 2, 292–301.

IV. How to choose the right approach for your child

Interdisciplinary Council on Developmental and Learning Disorders (ICDL) (2003) *Clinical Practice Guidelines*. ICDL and Dr. Stanley Greenspan, pubs., supported by Unicorn Children's Foundation, Bethesda, MD. Available at www.icdl.com/dirFloortime/ClinicalPracticeGuidelines/ClinicalPracticeGuidelines.shtml.

V. Selected personal accounts of life with autism

Grandin, T. (1996) *Thinking in Pictures and Other Reports From My Life with Autism*. New York: Vintage Books.

Higashida, N. (2007) (trans. K.A. Yoshida and David Mitchell) *The Reason I Jump: The Inner Voice of a Thirteen-Year-Old Boy with Autism*. New York: Random House.

Lawson, W. (2000) *Life Behind Glass: A Personal Account of Autism Spectrum Disorder*. London: Jessica Kingsley Publishers.

MacElwain, J. and Paisner, D. (2009) *The Game of My Life: A True Story of Challenge, Triumph, and Growing Up Autistic*. New York: NAL Penguin.

Martin, R. (1995) *Out of Silence: An Autistic Boy's Journey into Language and Communication*. New York: Penguin.

Mukhopadhyay, T.R. (2001) *The Mind Tree: A Miraculous Child Breaks the Silence of Autism*. New York: Arcade Publishing.

Mukhopadhyay, T.R. (2011) *How Can I Talk if My Lips Don't Move?: Inside My Autistic Mind*. New York: Arcade Publishing.

Pacelli, T. (2012) *Six-Word Lessons on Growing Up Autistic: 100 Lessons to Understand How Autistic People See Life*. Leading on the Edge International. Available at http://project-management-books.com.

Shore, S. (2001) *Beyond the Wall: Personal Experiences with Autism and Asperger Syndrome*. Shawnee Mission, Kansas: Autism Asperger Publishing Company.

Williams, D. (1994) *Somebody Somewhere: Breaking Free from the World of Autism*. New York: Times Books.

VI. Sources of inspiration

Garcia Marquez, G. (2003) *Vivir Para Contarla*. New York: Vintage.

Hammer, R. (2005) *Entering the High Holy Days: A Complete Guide to the History, Prayers and Themes*. Philadelphia: Jewish Publication Society.

INDEX

SPEED DIAL INDEX
FOR PROMPT HELP

For the healing of the world
םלוע ןוקית
TIKKUN OLAM